REMARKABLE
BICYCLE RIDES

First published in the United Kingdom in 2021 by
Pavilion Books,
43 Great Ormond Street,
London WC1N 3HZ

Produced by Salamander Editorial
Part of the Remarkable series which includes
Remarkable Cricket Grounds, *Remarkable Golf Courses*,
Remarkable Racecourses, *Remarkable Village Cricket
Grounds* and *Remarkable Road Trips*.

Picture research: Hetty Hopkinson

ISBN 978-1-911641-42-1

A CIP catalogue record for this book is available from
the British Library.

10 9 8 7 6 5 4 3 2 1

Reproduction by Rival UK

Printed and bound by 1010 Printing International,
China

Photo Credits
All images supplied by Alamy

Cover photo: An alpine panorama, with a trail heading
through the Jungfrau region of Switzerland.

Contents page: Close to the edge on the White Rim
Trail in the Canyonlands National Park, Utah.

Page 224: The end of the Fisher Towers trail above the
Colorado River in Professor Valley near Moab, Utah.

REMARKABLE
BICYCLE RIDES

COLIN SALTER

PAVILION

Contents

Introduction

It's estimated that more than half of the world's population can ride a bike, compared to around 17% who *think* they can drive a car. Concern for the environment, cost, and increased consideration for cycling in urban planning have all contributed to the rise in bike use.

Giant strides have been made in the provision of cycling infrastructure within towns and cities. Separate bicycle lanes with their own traffic signals are common, and commuting to work by bicycle is a much safer proposition today than it was twenty years ago. The more people cycle to work, the fewer people drive to work, the cleaner the air is for those who cycle (or walk) to work.

Cycling is a tremendously efficient way of getting from A to B over short to medium distances. In built-up areas it's faster than driving; and the parking is infinitely easier. It's ideal for commuting. Better still, that short ride to work every day is a far more effective way of keeping fit than an occasional longer route.

But cycling is addictive. You find yourself wanting the longer route at the weekend as well as the daily work-out. It's as if those lungs, once opened, want all the fresh air they can get. Those legs, once accustomed to pedalling, must pedal.

In reality, most of us stop before things get too extreme – the 1,220km of Chile's Carretera Austral across volcanoes, fjords and glaciers is not for everyone. A family cycling holiday along the banks of the River Loire is a far gentler proposition. A day out every now and then – for example Oregon's 33-mile Crater Lake Loop around a single volcano – would satisfy me and most of my fellow weekend cyclists. (In this book,

by the way, we use the local units of distance first, be they kilometres or miles, metres or feet)

But whether you're planning to ride the Great Divide or just dreaming of the Shimanami Kaido, this book offers an armchair taster of 53 remarkable bike rides from around the world to whet your appetite. They vary in length, from the short sharp shock of the Whistler A-Line Singletrack (one and a half miles and five minutes you'll never forget) to the seven-country, 6,000 kilometre coastal extravaganza of the North Sea Cycle Route. They vary in altitude and gradient too, from the level paths of the Dutch coast to the lung-busting twists and turns of the Mount Evans Climb in Colorado.

There's something within every cyclist that loves a challenge. Although many of us think a steep hill spoils an otherwise enjoyable ride, others crave the punishment of a 20% incline. There's plenty for them in here. The French version of the Camino de Santiago has to cross the Pyrenean Mountains, while in Scotland, the Assynt and Applecross Circuits make no effort to take the low road through the rugged Scottish Highlands. The Alpine Panorama Route through Switzerland crosses four different mountain ranges and in Cuba, La Farola crosses the island's spine on a marvel of mountain road engineering.

It's not always the ascent that's the hard part: the Yungas Road in Bolivia can be ridden downhill all the way but clings to mountains so steep that it is known with good reason as the Road of Death.

RIGHT: Two cyclists tackle the short but steep climb of the Wrynose Pass in England's Lake District.

Some of the most challenging climbs in cycling are part of its greatest competitions. Mont Ventoux is a regular component of the Tour de France, the Stelvio Pass a favourite in the Italian equivalent, the Giro d'Italia, while Tuscany's L'Eroica is both a race and a celebration of the joys of vintage cycling in the kind of kit Fausto Coppi would have donned.

For the flat-earthers among us, who prefer a less strenuous route, riverside paths and railroad beds offer a pleasant escape from the ups and downs of the landscape, and of life. In Europe, Germany leads the way, with some 37 designated cycle routes along its rivers, including the Elbe, the Rhine, the Main and the upper reaches of the Danube. If you have the time you can follow the Danube for its entire 2,850km length from spring to mouth through ten countries and four capital cities. Parts of it form sections of many other long-distance cycle routes including the excellent EuroVelo network promoted by the European Union. Several EVs are described in whole or in part in this book, including the 7,600km Iron Curtain Trail, EuroVelo 13, which follows the continent's sparsely populated former boundaries between Capitalism and Communism.

Railways have even more reliable gradients than riverbanks and, when they close down, rail travel's loss is the cyclist's gain. The Otago Central Rail Trail in New Zealand and Le P'tit Train du Nord in Canada, having outlived their usefulness to the local gold and timber

ABOVE LEFT: Cycle tours can help take the organizational strain, but you will always need to travel at the group speed and stick to a predetermined plan.

LEFT: A cyclist on the Great North Trail passing through the Yorkshire Dales.

OPPOSITE: The Route of the Hiawatha accomplishes a rare feat. Cyclists can enjoy an exhilarating ride in mountainous country, while pedalling on the flat.

industries, now serve weekend cyclists instead, carrying more people now than they ever did in their lifetimes. The Parenzana, once the rail link between Italy and Croatia, does even more. It has been repurposed as a bike trail to reconnect two countries once separated by ideologies. The USA is justly proud of its 'Rails to Trails' scheme and two of its most popular rails – the Route of the Hiawatha and the Katy Trail – are featured here.

The Katy Trail follows the Missouri river and passes the city of Hermann, the self-styled Sausage Capital of Missouri: it's not always about the cycling. Besides the mountains, the Swiss Alpine Panoramic Route also encompasses several of the country's world-famous cheese-making towns. There are many cycling circuits in Flanders dedicated to the region's prowess at brewing beer. And in Burgundy you can follow the Route des Grands Crus for a finely judged balance – and balance is an important thing here – of cycling and wine-tasting.

If your sea legs are as strong as your cycling legs, you may enjoy a spot of island-hopping. Island communities often have their own values and lifestyles, and in this book we look at four archipelagos which can be explored by bike via ferries or bridges, in Norway, Japan, Scotland and Washington State.

One of the greatest advantages of cycling is the ability to travel under your own steam and set your own pace. Unlike cars, most of a bike's mechanical problems can be fixed at the roadside. The logical extension of this self-sufficiency is one of the great long-distance trails included in this book. A pair of bicycle panniers will easily hold a toolkit, a tent, a sleeping bag and a change of underwear. The only other thing you need a lot of is time.

The 1,000km Munda Biddi Trail across the south-western corner of Australia passes signs of civilization only once every 100km or so. The Great Divide, the North American watershed from which water flows either to the Pacific or to the Atlantic Ocean, is a 2,800-mile epic adventure from Canada to the Mexican border. It can be done in thirteen days, although mere mortals are more likely to take six to ten weeks over it.

Whether you are serious about undertaking any of the rides in this collection, or are just serious about reading about them, enjoy the rides. It is more true of cycling than of most other forms of transport, that it is far better to travel well than to arrive.

Colin Salter
Spring 2021

Adige Cycle Path

Italy

Length: 187 km, 116 miles
Start: Reschen Pass
Finish: Trento
Highlights: Graun Church, Glurns/Glorenza, Churburg Castle, Juval Castle, Vigiljoch Cable Car, Iceman Ötzi, Bozen Victory Monument, Runkelstein Castle, Sigmundskron Castle, Haderburg Castle, Salorno Bicigrill, Trento Medieval Centre

A section of the ancient Via Claudia Augusta descends through South Tyrol in northern Italy. The region is a fusion of Italian and German culture and beside the magnificent castle-studded alpine scenery it has the great advantage of being downhill all the way.

The Via Claudia Augusta was the first Roman road to cross the Alps. It was a vital imperial artery connecting Italy with Rhaetia (modern-day southern Germany). It originally ran from Hostiliae (a trade hub in the Po Valley) to Augusta Vindelicorum, a garrison camp which shows its Roman origins in its modern name, Augsburg. Later it was extended to Sumuntorium, a Roman outpost near modern-day Donauwörth on the Danube. This link between two major rivers (Po and Danube) boosted the exchange of international goods and ideas as well as facilitating Rome's control of its northern provinces.

Today the route is a popular long-distance cycle trail, with a single route through Germany and Austria, and variations in Italy to either Ostiglia

or Venice. It's generally well signposted as the VCA and mostly follows traffic-free paths or quiet roads. But please note that bicycles are banned from the centre of Venice – you can't even push them along without risking a €100 fine. The full route, up to 713 km long, is well served by bike shuttle services.

Very roughly speaking the VCA follows the River Lech in Germany and the River Inn in Austria before crossing into Italy on the Reschen Pass. In Italian South Tyrol, German is still the predominant language and you will often see bilingual signs. Just below the pass on the Italian side is the Reschensee/Lago di Résia (Lake Resia). At its head is the Schöneben/Comprensorio ski and MTB complex and the VCA runs either side of the lake. You will see the forlorn steeple of the old church at Graun sticking out of the water; it was left there when the Reschen reservoir was created in 1953.

On your left are the Ötztal Alps, where the body of a 5,300-year-old man nicknamed Ötzi was discovered in a glacier in 1991. The route

TOP RIGHT: Lake Reschen with its sunken church tower.

ABOVE RIGHT: A pedestrianized street in the fortified village of Glorenza, one of the most beautiful villages in Italy.

RIGHT: The medieval castle of Churburg in the village of Schluderns in Vinschgau, South Tyrol.

OPPOSITE: Looking down on the water and terraced garden of Trauttmansdorff Castle near Merano, South Tyrol.

descends in a series of lazy hairpins past the imposing Marienburg Monastery (Abbazia Monte Maria) to Mals/Malles. Mals is the local centre of population and the nearest you can get to the Reschenpass by train. Just south of Mals is Glurns/Glorenza, Italy's smallest city, with its impressive defensive walls.

Here the route meets the Adige/Etsch river for the first time and its upper valley is known as the Vinschgau. The rainfall is lower than average in the Vinschgau and for centuries locals have irrigated their orchards and vines with channels from the Adige. South of the village are the well-preserved buildings of the Churburg, a thirteenth-century castle. Castles punctuate the Vinschgau, and Juval Castle at Schnals/Senales is accessible only by a tunnel through the rock.

After a string of pretty villages, the first significant town on the route is Meran/Merano, which sits at a bend in the Vinschgau where the Adige is joined by the Passer/Passirio river. Meran grew from a road station on the VCA to become the capital of the Tyrol. Its mild climate made it a favourite of Empress Elizabeth of Austria in the nineteenth century and today it is known for its spa, its wine and its attractive old centre.

South of Meran the signed route is along the Via Roma, although you can also travel on the west side of the valley through Marling/Marlengo, from which there's a cable car to the Vigiljoch mountain above the town. Near Marling, the village of Lana is one of only three which weren't renamed after South Tyrol was transferred to Italy after World War I; it was deemed Italian enough already because the town ended with a vowel.

Here the Adige flows through the Dolomite mountains, named after the mineral which occurs in high proportion in their limestone. In Italy the annual one-day Maratona dles Dolomites road race, open to amateur cyclists, follows a route over seven Dolomite peaks.

The city of Bozen/Bolzano is the largest in South Tyrol, a crossroads of the Italian and Austro-German cultures of the region. Iceman Ötzi is displayed in a museum here. Bozen is architecturally rich, not only in Gothic and Romanesque styles but also in two buildings

TOP: Castel Lebenberg in Marlengo (Marling).

ABOVE LEFT: One of cycling's Grand Tours, the Giro d'Italia passes through San Candido.

ABOVE RIGHT: Castel Roncolo near Bolzano (Bozen) is famed for its ancient frescoes.

erected by Mussolini – the neoclassical Victory Monument (1928) and the rationalist Casa del Fascio (1942), the former headquarters of the Italian Fascist Party. Just outside the city are two splendid medieval castles, Schloss Runkelstein (Castel Roncolo) and Schloss Sigmundskron (Ponte d'Adige).

After Bozen the Adige's youthful mountain energy is to some extent over. It now makes its way at a more stately pace through the fertile Adige Valley. At Salorno (one of only five places in South Tyrol with an Italian-speaking majority) the valley walls briefly crowd in. Here Haderburg Castle guards the route from a rocky outcrop halfway up the mountain.

At Salorno too you'll find an example of a feature of the Italian cycle network, the 'Bicigrill'. Inspired by the Autogrills in rest areas on Italian motorways, these are small but welcome cafés alongside cycle paths. Salorno marks the

southern end of the Vinschgau. Beyond it you enter the Trentino district. The next town, Lavis, has a beautiful historic centre and a museum dedicated to the local Moser family, who produced nine cycling champions. They include the legendary Francesco Moser, who won the Giro d'Italia in 1984. Visits are by appointment.

Trento, exuberantly Italian, marks the end of this section of the Via Claudia Augusta. Its old centre includes the thirteenth-century Castello Buonconsiglio, a fourteenth-century cathedral built over a sixth-century church, and the fifteenth-century Palazzo Geremia. Trento has launched a new vintage bicycle race modelled on L'Eroica in Tuscany called the Moserissima, in honour of Lavis' favourite sons. From Trento you can choose to continue to the original terminus of the VCA at Ostiglia or to head for Venice. The Adige and the Po eventually enter the Adriatic Sea side by side in the Po delta, without ever actually meeting.

ABOVE LEFT: A view of the historic town of Trento from Castel Buonconsiglio.

ABOVE: The 18th-century Neptune Fountain in Piazzo Duomo in Trento.

Alpine Panorama Route

Switzerland

Length: 478 km, 297 miles
Start: St Margrethen
Finish: Aigle
Highlights: Braunwaldbahn, Klausenpass, Bürglen, Lake Lucerne steamer and ferry, Stans, Glaubenbielenpass, Sörenberg, Schangnau, Thun, Schwarzenburg, Fribourg, Cailler chocolate factory, Gruyères, Hongrin, Col d'Ayerne

Not all of Switzerland is mountainous, but this route crosses three mountain ranges on its way from the Rhine to the Rhône. Along the way there are all the ingredients for a perfect Swiss holiday – cheese, chocolate, cows, mountains, lakes … and William Tell.

Switzerland is criss-crossed by nine national long-distance cycle routes, covering the entire country. Number 4, the Alpine Panorama Route, goes from its north-eastern border with Austria to its south-western corner near the border with France. It connects the country's two major bodies of water, Lake Constance and Lake Geneva, and the two European rivers, the Rhine and the Rhône, which rise within 25 km of each other in the eastern Swiss Alps. The route is well signposted, mostly on minor roads with some farm tracks and traffic-free sections. A touring bike will be up to the challenge if you are.

St Margrethen is the last Swiss town through which the Rhine flows before entering Lake Constance (known locally in German-speaking northern Switzerland as the Bodensee). Like many major rivers, the Rhine has often been on the front line. Germany lies on the far side of the Bodensee, Austria at the other end of the only bridge across the Rhine here; and just south of St Margrethen the river forms the Switzerland-Liechtenstein border.

The Alpine Panorama Route heads away from the river towards the heart of Switzerland. The route is divided into eight stages, each relatively short but all quite hilly. The first crosses the rolling farmland of the historic canton of Appenzell,

famous for its dry wit and strong local dialect. These are the foothills of Säntis (2,502 metres/ 8,209 ft), the highest and most visible mountain of the Appenzeller Alps. The stage ends in the charming narrow streets of the village of Appenzell. Since the sixteenth century, on the last Sunday of every April, its citizens have been required by law to attend a meeting in the village square to choose their rulers. In 1991 it was the last canton in Switzerland to give women a vote on local issues.

ABOVE: A wide panorama in Appenzellerland, Switzerland, looking across to the distant Säntis mountain.

RIGHT: Typical valley floor cycling in the Alps.

The second stage climbs from Appenzell on the Sitter river up the Kaubach stream and down the swelling Chronbach river to its merger with the Urnäsch. The '-bach' placename element means 'stream'. The gradients are a little gentler here, but the land becomes more rugged and forested. From Urnäsch, it's up and over to the Necker Valley, then the Thur, and then the Rickenbach. At last the road drops down to the wide, flat plain of Glaster, and follows the icy blue River Linth to Glarus, the end of this section of the Route.

Glarus speaks a dialect variation of Swiss-German, and has a grand, castellated railway station. Two-thirds of the town's buildings in Glarus were destroyed by a fire in 1861. The flames were fanned by the Föhn wind, a blast of hot air from the Mediterranean which can raise temperatures by up to 14°C in a few hours.

The next stage follows the railway and the Linth upstream as the valley narrows. Just after Rüti a funicular railway built in 1907 connects the valley floor with the car-free village of Braunwald 650 metres (2,133 ft) above. Cyclists must climb twice as high on the road to the summit of the Klausenpass (1,948 metres/6,391 ft), beginning with a ladder of eight hairpin bends. After following the high Urnerboden valley to its end, another ten hairpins take you to the top. The Urnerboden is the highest pasture alp in Switzerland and the views are as breathtaking as the ride. The pass is closed from October to May.

The descent clings to the vertiginous sides of the Schächen valley, and the pretty village of Bürglen at the bottom is a welcome sight. It's the birthplace of the legendary Swiss folk hero William Tell and a chapel is dedicated to him. Just around the corner is Flüelen, on the

ABOVE LEFT: Giving it a lot of cowbell on the Klausenpass-Strasse near Urnerboden.

TOP: Looking back down the valley from near the top of the Klausenpass.

ABOVE: The church at Beckenried with Lake Lucerne beyond.

southern shore of Lake Lucerne, the end of this third stage of the Alpine Panorama Route.

When travelling by boat was easier than travelling overland (and after the Klausenpass you'll appreciate that), Flüelen was an important trading post. Today it's still a steamer terminal for services to Lucerne. Officially the cycle route follows the old shore road north from here, but this is one of the busiest roads on the trail, and although there are bicycle lanes they sometimes form part of the highway. Cyclists are advised to take the train, or the steamer, between Flüelen and Brunnen; and the steamer makes a pleasant change of pace as it threads its way between the mountain tops. At Gersau, a few kilometres beyond Brunnen, you have to take to the water again to cross the lake by ferry to Beckenried.

Now the route follows the south-western shore of the lake. The pretty village square of Stans owes

ABOVE: Cafes aplenty on the lakefront at Brunnen on the north shore of Lake Lucerne.

its Baroque appearance to another disastrous fire, this one in 1713, after which the town's buildings were erected in the prevailing style of the time. Here the route leaves Lake Lucerne and works along a chain of small lakes to Sarnen.

Sarnen has been an important staging post for centuries, commanding the Glaubenbielenpass to the west. The Alpine Panorama Route must cross this pass, on a zig-zagging road known as the Panoramastrasse. Eleven hairpin bends take you from Giswil at the bottom to the summit 1,100 metres (3,609 ft) higher, on gradients of up to 12% through the trees to alpine pastures. The views of Giswilerstock, the mountain on whose flanks you ride, are stupendous and the descent to Sörenberg not nearly as precarious as the ascent.

Sörenberg with its pretty onion-domed church tower marks the end of the fourth stage. It lies in the shadow of the Brienzer Rothorn (2,350 metres/7,710 ft), the highest mountain in the Emmental Alps through which you have been travelling. A cable car from the village to the summit means you don't have to cycle up it.

After a short incline out of Sörenberg, the next stage is a welcome descent with the Emme river, at the foot of the Schrattenflue chain of mountains, to Schangnau, a charming chocolate-box Swiss village. The Emme Valley gives its name to Emmental cheese. Beyond a covered wooden bridge over the river, the route veers away, with a snaking ascent of the Schallenberg Pass – maximum gradient 10%. Then it's downhill or flat as you ride by pastures and timber houses all the way to Thun, the end of the section.

ABOVE LEFT: There's plenty of summer accommodation to be had in the ski village of Sörenberg.

LEFT: A typical Alpine meadow at Schangnau in early summer.

Thun, where the River Aare pours out of Lake Thun, has been a strategically important site since the Stone Age; its twelfth-century towering fortress still dominates the town. Trips on the paddle steamer Blüemlisalp leave from here, and you can see three iconic Swiss mountains to the south: the Eiger, the Mönch and the Jungfrau.

From Thun the next section is a series of small ups and downs – the climb up to alpine Burgistein not *quite* so small – through woodland and scattered villages. Schwarzenburg is so pretty that the entire village has been designated a Swiss Heritage Site. Soon after it you cross the River Sense from German-speaking Switzerland into an area which is predominantly French. Fribourg, the end of this section, has one of the largest preserved medieval centres in Europe, with surviving defensive walls, several fine bridges over the River Sarine and a multitude of fountains in its squares.

ABOVE: A grand view from the ramparts of Spiez Castle looking down on Lake Thun.

RIGHT: The River Sarine passing through Fribourg.

The Sarine twists back and forth, and the route beyond Fribourg does its best to follow it upstream past the Abbaye d'Hauterive and the ruined castles of Arconciel and Illens, which face each other in the folds of an S-shaped gorge. Road and river finally meet at the Rossens dam, behind which lies the Lac de la Gruyère. In Broc at the southern end of the lake – at last – there's that essential ingredient of any Swiss holiday, a chocolate factory, originally for the Cailler brand and now part of the Nestlé group.

Next, more Swiss iconography: just above Broc stands the medieval hill town of Gruyères, where the cheese comes from. Like Schwarzenburg the whole town is a Heritage Site, with a cheese factory in neighbouring Pringy and a handsome castle. A short detour from the route takes you to Moléson-sur-Gruyères, from which a cable car goes to the top of the imposing Moléson mountain peak. The stage ends with a long, gentle rise along the upper reaches of the Sarine

to the village of Montbovon, at the head of the Lac de Lessoc through which the river passes. Look out for a house called Croix-Blanche, a former inn with an ornate carved wooden façade.

The final section of the Alpine Panorama Route climbs steadily from Montbovon up the remote Hongrin valley to the twin arcs of the hydroelectric Hongrin dam. The road curls around the reservoir through the Forêt de Charbonnières, 'Coal Forest'. This is an area often used for military exercises. The route climbs steadily on the Col d'Ayerne, a pass between the mountains of Les Rochers de Naye and Tour d'Aï.

The summit, at 1,555 metres (5,102 ft), with views of Lake Geneva far below, is the start of an uninterrupted descent of over 1,150 metres (3,773 ft), through tunnels and around hairpins to

BELOW: An aerial view of Hauterive Abbey in a meander carved out by the River Sarine near Fribourg.

LEFT TOP: The Alpenpanorama Route (National Cycle Route 4) winding through the Sarine Valley near Neirivue.

LEFT MIDDLE: Famous for its cheese, the ancient village of Gruyères.

LEFT BOTTOM: Surfaces on the route vary, as this gravel track near Montbovon shows.

BELOW: The castle and museum at Aigle in the canton of Vaud, fittingly surrounded by vineyards.

the floor of the Rhône valley. The town of Aigle comes on you almost abruptly at the end of this exhilarating gravity ride. Aigle has a grand castle that houses a Museum of the Vine. But right now, you're probably more interested in drinking the stuff than learning about its history.

The Applecross Loop

Scotland

Length: 43 miles, 69 km
Start/Finish: The Bealach Café
Highlights: Bealach na Bà, Applecross, Raasay, Ob Chuaig, Shieldaig, Lochcarron

Until the early twentieth century, Applecross was accessible only by boat, cut off from the rest of the Scottish mainland by a mountain barrier. Now there are two roads in and out and, as any cyclist knows, two roads make a circuit.

You can get to Applecross the long way, following the coast, or the short way, over a perilous mountain road called Bealach na Bà – 'the Pass of the Cattle'. The short way is only 11 miles from the nearest main road to the Applecross Inn; the coastal road is three times that, but probably won't take you much longer. Together, however, they add up to a very satisfying balance of big climbs, level roads and magnificent scenery, with views across the sea to the glorious Isle of Skye.

The nearest main road is the A896 between Lochcarron and Shieldaig. Both villages have accommodation, and Lochcarron is only four miles from Strathcarron station on the scenic railway line from Inverness to Kyle of Lochalsh.

Six miles north of Lochcarron in Tornapress, a small sign beside the Bealach Café points you to a harmless-looking side road. Once you've turned off, however, the signs tell a different story: 'Road normally impassable in wintry conditions', 'Gradients of 1 in 5 and hairpin bends', 'Not advised for learner drivers, very large vehicles or caravans after the first mile'. You can't say you weren't warned. From this point just above sea level, the road – barely wider than the axles of a small family car – winds its way up to

more than 2,000 ft (610 metres) over the next six miles, like something in the Swiss Alps. It then descends to the shore at Applecross over only five miles. Test your brakes.

The village at Applecross is a popular day out for holidaymakers in the area. There's a stony beach, and echoes of the monastery established here in AD 672 by St Maelrubha, an Irish monk. Across the sea here lies the island of Raasay with its distinctive flat-topped highpoint Dun Caan, and beyond that the high Cuillin Mountains of Skye. The Sound is the deepest stretch of sea in Britain's territorial waters, and the Royal Navy uses it for submarine tests. You may see one on the surface.

The return route from Applecross is the meandering, undulating coastal road, which hugs the western and northern shores of the Applecross peninsula. This road, a vital lifeline in winter, was only built in the 1970s. Near the northern tip it's a short walk to Ob Chuaig, a deserted pebble bay with a sea cave accessible at low tide. The more sheltered north-east coast is home to a scattered farming and fishing community along the side of Loch Shieldaig, and when you rejoin the main road it's left for the village of Shieldaig, or right for Lochcarron and the Bealach Café from where you started.

OPPOSITE TOP AND BOTTOM LEFT: Two views of the Bealach na Bà pass.

OPPOSITE BOTTOM RIGHT: Bealach na Bà is Britain's longest continuous ascent road.

TOP RIGHT: The Applecross Inn facing Applecross Bay.

MIDDLE RIGHT: A cottage on the shores of Loch Shieldaig.

RIGHT: The view across Loch Shieldaig to the Torridon Mountains.

Assynt Circuit

Scotland

Length: 73 miles, 117 km
Start/Finish: Achiltibuie
Highlights: Stac Pollaidh, Inverkirkaig, Suilven, Lochinver, Clachtoll Beach, Quinag, Glas Bheinn, Canisp, Ben More Assynt, Ardvreck Castle, Elphin, Ben More Coigach

A circuit through the oldest mountains in Britain takes you past lochs and castles, along sea shores and over winding passes – the essential Scottish Highlands.

Half the roads on the Assynt Circuit won't show up on maps drawn at smaller scales, so far off the beaten track are they. Achiltibuie, on the northern shore of Loch Broom, sits almost at the end of one of them, so far from anywhere that it still supports a local shop and petrol pump. There's a youth hostel here, and the village's hotel, named after the Summer Isles archipelago just offshore, has an excellent reputation for locally caught seafood.

Nothing is straightforward about this route. Although the village is only 8.5 miles from the main road as the crow flies, it's 17.5 miles by winding humpback road around the lochs and mountains of the Coigach peninsula. The road north from Achiltibuie to the fishing harbour at Lochinver takes such an indirect route that it's known to locals as the Wee Mad Road. The rocks here are the oldest in Britain, from a time when it was still connected to eastern Canada; it's a chaotic landscape torn this way and that by ancient geological faults, and large parts of Assynt have been declared a geopark.

A map of Assynt shows more water than land – hundreds of lochs and interconnecting streams. The mountains display an extraordinary variety of forms – pointed, rounded, flat-topped, hogbacked. Stac Pollaidh and Suilven seem to rise up from nowhere.

Soon after leaving Lochinver, the route turns left onto a minor road for Clachtoll and Clashnessie, two fine and unexpected sandy beaches in these rocky surroundings. There are ups and downs as the road hops from cove to cove, while the three-spurred mountain Quinag towers above. If you're lucky you'll see wild red deer along the way, and perhaps even a golden eagle.

At a junction the route turns south over the pass between Quinag and Glas Bheinn ('green mountain') and meets the main Lochinver road on the shore of Loch Assynt. Across the water is distinctive Canisp, and to the left the king of the summits here, Ben More Assynt, 'the great mountain of Assynt'.

Turning right again at a junction, you pass through the community of Elphin, which refused to be dispersed when its nineteenth-century landlords wanted to clear the land for sheep and sport. Beyond Elphin there's a gruelling 3-mile ascent, and when you take the turn to Achiltibuie there are still those 17.5 undulating miles to go, between the twin peaks of Cùl Mòr and Ben More Coigach.

Little by little the road steps down past five lochs back to Achiltibuie. The scenery throughout this circuit is unrivalled in Britain. The road surfaces are good and the climbs, although occasionally severe, are usually short. There are few opportunities for refreshment along the route. If you are rehydrating in either of Achiltibuie's bars afterwards, the toast is *Slàinte mhath!* ('Good health', pronounced slan-jeh vah.)

TOP: Stuck for a signal? You can phone home from Lochinver.

MIDDLE: Ruined Ardvreck Castle sits on the shore of Loch Assynt.

ABOVE: Scattered crofts at Elphin.

OPPOSITE: The wee-mad-road heading towards Canisp and Suilven.

The Barry Way

Australia

Length: 170 km, 106 miles
Start: Jindabyne, NSW
Finish: Buchan, Victoria
Highlights: Snowy River, Suggan Buggan River, W-Tree Falls, Murrindal Cave Reserve

You better be sure you know what you're doing before you set off on the Barry Way. There are no towns along its route, no services except the occasional campground, not even another road. You do this ride for the wide wilderness and majestic mountains.

Jindabyne moved to its present location when the dam holding Jindabyne Reservoir was built in the 1960s. In the summer it's a great place for water sports, and in the winter it services the nearby skiing resorts of the appropriately named Snowy Mountains. In spring and autumn, when the weather is relatively temperate, it's the starting point for the Barry Way.

The route, intended as a useful shortcut across the south-eastern corner of Australia, was a long time coming. It was prompted by the building of a bridge over the Buchan River in 1925, and initially constructed entirely by pick and shovel during the Great Depression. World War II interrupted its progress, and councillor Leo Barry revived the scheme in the 1950s. It was finally opened in 1961.

The road is paved for the first 27 km, as far as Ingebirah Gap. Thereafter it's a dusty dirt track through the bush, and downhill virtually all the way to the NSW/VIC border. Eventually it runs alongside Jacob's River, where it flows into the Snowy River. A campground here is the first of three before the Victoria border.

In Victoria, the Barry Road becomes the Snowy River Road, and after a few kilometres it leaves the Snowy River to climb over to the Suggan Buggan valley. The simple plank bridge over the Suggan Buggan River marks the extent of construction of the Barry Road before the war. Beside the river a ghost village of wooden houses includes a schoolhouse built in 1865, which still has its desk and benches.

The stiffest ascent of the route takes the twisting track away from Suggan Buggan up to the Wulgulmerang. It comes as a bit of a shock to find a paved surface again, arriving from McKillop's Bridge. With big views to the left and right the trail now descends in easy stages along Butcher's Ridge.

The scenic W-Tree Falls at the roadside mark the start of the W-Tree Falls Scenic Reserve around the Murrindal River, and a little further on the Murrindal Cave Reserve. This is limestone country and there is a cluster of caves open to the public between here and the trail end at Buchan Cave Reserve Visitor Centre. In Buchan, you'll be pleased to hear, accommodation, refreshments and health services are available for the dusty, thirsty cyclist.

OPPOSITE: The upper reaches of the Snowy River as it flows alongside the Barry Way.

LEFT: Suggan Buggan's Old Schoolhouse.

Cabot Trail

Cape Breton, Canada

Length: 296 km, 184 miles
Start/Finish: Baddeck
Highlights: Alexander Graham Bell Museum, Ingonish, Neil's Harbour, North Mountain, whale watching, MacKenzie Mountain, Margaree River, the Lakes O'Law (First, Second and Third)

The Cabot Trail is named after Italian sailor John Cabot, in 1497 the first European to discover North America. Although historians now believe he landed on Newfoundland, not Cape Breton, the trail is a great way to see Canada past and present by bike.

Cape Breton is separated from the rest of Nova Scotia by the Strait of Canso, and by the ambitions of Angus L. Macdonald, who set out to promote tourism to his home island. Born in Cape Breton and of unsurprisingly Scottish descent, Angus focused on the Scottish heritage of the area, although, as the name implies, the island also has strong French connections. Like the rest of Canada, Nova Scotia ('New Scotland') was opened up by settlers from both countries. It's why Canada remains officially bilingual today.

Macdonald devised the Cabot Trail, which was constructed in 1932 and surrounds the northern third of the island. Navigating the wild coastline, it includes some steep climbs and descents, linking the small communities which make their living from the sea and from tourism. The trail quickly caught the public's imagination and became a popular day trip for motoring families. Recently it has been upgraded for the benefit of cyclists, with new stretches of paved bicycle lanes, new bicycle stands, and signage about gradients and sources of drinking water. The result is a touring route worth spending three or four days on.

The trail begins in Baddeck, the largest town in the area, whose population of 700 can double during the weeks of the holiday season. After taking a holiday here in 1885, Scottish inventor Alexander Graham Bell returned the following year to build a new home and laboratories. When he died in 1922 he was buried nearby in a coffin made of Cape Breton pine. Best known for inventing the telephone, it was in Cape Breton that he flew the first aeroplane to fly in the British Empire, and here that he tested his experimental hydrofoil. Baddeck has a museum dedicated to his work.

It's best to tackle the route in an anticlockwise direction. This puts you on the seaward side of the road, with the best views, although with some steep drops it may not suit riders of a nervous disposition. Heading east from Baddeck on Highway 105 the trail soon turns left and crosses St Ann's Peninsula, where Angus L. Macdonald established the *Colaisde na Gàidhlig*, The Gaelic College, to promote the language and culture of the Scottish Highlands, echoing the drive in the home country to rekindle the language with dual language English/Gaelic road signs.

The trail winds around the western shore of St Ann's Harbour before cutting overland to meet the open ocean on the east coast of Cape Breton. This coast is characterized by shallow inlets like Breton Cove and Wreck Cove – on these shores Atlantic winter storms have piled up the shingle beaches to make dams, trapping rainwater in brackish ponds.

Sandy beaches alternate with rocky outcrops and after Wreck Cove there is a challenging ascent of the slopes of Smokey Mountain, with gradients

OPPOSITE: A view of Cape Smokey from Middle Head.

BELOW: Baddeck Lighthouse. Baddeck is the home of the Alexander Graham Bell National Historic Site.

of 12% to 15%, before you return to the coast at Ingonish. Ingonish is a popular holiday centre with two wide sandy bays, South Bay and North Bay, separated by Middle Head, where there are some delightful walks. Some of the earliest settlers made their landfall here.

Others arrived further north. They were French, but the place where they landed is now called Neil's Harbour after Neil McLennan, a Scot who made the sheltered bay his home. Neil's Harbour is home to one of the Cabot Trail's must-visit attractions, the Chowder House restaurant. From Neil's Harbour the trail turns north-west, crossing overland to the contrarily named South Harbour. A spur from the main route will take you to the northernmost shore of Cape Breton – Cape North, where the battered remains of concrete buildings are evidence of the sea's potential for ferocity.

The trail proper now crosses over to the west coast on a string of short, sharp ascents and descents ranging up to 15%, across the flanks of North Mountain. There is respite at Pleasant Bay, a good whale-watching centre, before the road turns south and climbs again, across MacKenzie

Mountain and French Mountain with gradients of up to 12%. From the heart of the Cape Breton Highlands National Park it then drops sharply back to the sea. In the shadow of Jerome Mountain, a high point on the road south gives a great view up and down the coast.

There is more evidence of French settlement in the place names here – Petit Étang, Chéticamp, Terre Noir, Belle Côte. Whale-watching cruises depart from Chéticamp, and beyond Belle Côte ('beautiful shore') the trail turns inland and follows the Margaree River upstream. The river is a good one for kayaking enthusiasts and anglers. At the Margaree Salmon Museum the route turns away from the river and soon afterwards begins its gradual descent back to Baddeck, passing the three Lakes O'Law and skirting Hunter's Mountain to land back at sea level just a few miles west of your starting point.

There are plenty of campsites and other forms of accommodation along the route, and enough settlements to ensure you need not carry too many provisions. The Cabot Trail is Canada in miniature. Its French and Scottish roots speak of Canada's past, and the combination of grand mountains and dramatic coastlines embodies all that's wonderful about the rugged Canadian landscape. It is a beautiful ride.

OPPOSITE: Neil's Harbour with a typical Cape Breton lighthouse beyond.

TOP: The road through North Mountain in the Cape Breton Highlands National Park.

ABOVE RIGHT: Cape Rouge is aptly named in the autumn, when the deciduous trees in the Nova Scotia forest turn glorious shades of rust, yellow and brown.

RIGHT: The Margaree River Valley.

Camino de Santiago

France, Portugal, Spain

Length: Up to 850 km, 528 miles
Start: Oviedo, Irun, Lisbon, Pass of Somport, Saint-Jean-Pied-de-Port
Finish: Santiago de Compostela
Highlights: Oviedo, Ponte de Lima, Saint-Jean-Pied-de-Port, Roncevaux Pass, Puente la Reina, León Cathedral, Casa Botines/Astorga Episcopal Palace, Villafranca del Bierzo, Alto de San Roque, Albergue Linar do Rei, Portomarín, Furelos, Santiago Cathedral

Pilgrims have been making their way to Santiago de Compostela since the bones of the apostle St James were discovered there in AD 813. Today more than 200,000 still make the journey annually. About 20,000 of them do so by bicycle.

The centre of Santiago in northern Spain is a UNESCO World Heritage Site for its architecture and religious significance. It is Spain's holiest place, dominated by the magnificent cathedral built on the spot where St James' remains were found. Whether you are a Christian pilgrim or just an enthusiastic cyclist, the deep spirituality of the place commands respect. And whether the journey to it tests your faith or your cycling endurance, it is a challenging one through some of western Europe's most beautiful countryside as well as its finest cities.

Pilgrims come from all over Europe, and several Pilgrims' Ways converge on Santiago. They were established over centuries, often passing through lesser holy sites on the way. Hostelries sprang up along the routes to cater for the travellers' needs, often run by holy orders of monks or nuns.

That tradition of hospitality persists along the Ways today. Travellers who hold a *credencial*, a sort of pilgrim passport, have access to a series of accredited pilgrim hostels which stamp their passport to show that they have passed along an official Camino. Cyclists with proof of a journey of 200 km or more are entitled to a certificate when they arrive in Santiago.

Most of the routes were firmly established by the thirteenth century. The oldest Way is the Camino Primitivo, the route followed by King Alfonso II, Alfonso the Chaste, in the ninth century soon after the discovery of the saint's relics. It begins in Oviedo, the Asturian capital in northern Spain.

Today much of the Primitivo is incorporated in the Camino del Norte, which follows Spain's north coast from Irun, on the border with France. The Camino del Norte, about 770 km in length, passes through Bilbao and Santander as well as Oviedo. It has a lot of ups and downs for cyclists, a tough route for which the compensations are spectacular views of the notoriously stormy Bay of Biscay.

ABOVE RIGHT: Oviedo Cathedral in Plaza Alfonso II, Oviedo.

RIGHT: San Vicente de la Barquera near Santander.

OPPOSITE: Porto in Portugal is another magnificent place to start a pilgrimage.

Another route, the Camino Portugues, approaches Santiago from the south through Portugal. It starts at Lisbon's cathedral and proceeds up the west coast of the Iberian Peninsula via Porto, or on an alternative route further inland. This is about 530 km long (280 km if you start from Porto) and one of the most popular Caminos. The inland route takes you through handsome towns less visited by tourists such as Barcelos, Ponte de Lima and Valença, where there is good infrastructure and less exposure to the vagaries of Atlantic weather fronts.

For pilgrims arriving from the rest of Europe there are a number of gathering points in

ABOVE: The river Nive running through Saint-Jean-Pied-de-Port with a backdrop of the Pyrenees.

northern and eastern France: Arles for those coming from Italy; Le Puy and Vézelay for Germanic and central European travellers; and Paris for the devout of northern Europe. From these centres all but the Arles Way converge on the border with Spain in the French province of Aquitaine.

The way from here is known as the Camino Frances and it follows a relatively level path inland across northern Spain to Santiago. Today this is the most popular Camino de Santiago, about 800 km from start to finish. Many people start in the small town of Saint-Jean-Pied-de-Port, a pretty settlement on the river Nive whose name means 'St John at the foot of the pass'.

ABOVE RIGHT: A towering view of the road in the French Pyrenees as it passes between Saint-Jean-Pied-de-Port and Roncevaux.

ABOVE FAR RIGHT: The route is signed with the distinctive Camino de Santiago logo.

RIGHT: Pilgrims Bridge at Puente la Reina.

BELOW: The former railway tunnel at Somport Pass adorned with Spanish and French flags.

To get from France to Spain you must cross the Pyrenean mountains, and Saint-Jean was where pilgrims gathered their strength before the Roncevaux Pass. This hairpin ascent – 900 metres (2,953 ft) over 18 km, averaging 5% – from the river and border crossing at Arnéguy is by far the hardest stretch of the Camino Frances for cyclists. At the 1,057-metre (3,468-ft) summit, Alto de Ibañeta, there is a modern chapel where you can give thanks for the magnificent views across the Pyrenees.

From there it's a long gradual descent to the cathedral city of Pamplona, famous today for its bull-running event in July, and the capital of the former Kingdom of Navarre. Pamplona is an elegant city with fine civic and religious architecture, built with the wealth brought by pilgrim traffic through it.

At Puente la Reina the Camino Frances is joined by the Camino Aragonés, which brings pilgrims and cyclists from Arles. That route crosses the Spanish border at the Pass of Somport, 50 km further east than Roncevaux, slightly higher and a harder ride too, crossing as it does the Hautes-Pyrénées, the High Pyrenees. From the 1,632-metre (5,354-ft) high point it drops down to the ancient walled city of Jaca, once capital of the Kingdom of Aragon.

Puente la Reina means 'the Queen's bridge', and here in the early eleventh century Queen Muniadona of Castile built a beautiful six-arched bridge for pilgrims to cross the Arga river on their way to Santiago. A thousand years later, the bridge still stands.

There's another important river crossing at Logroño, on the Ebro. The name means 'the

ABOVE LEFT: Puente de Piedra in Zaragoza.

LEFT: San Pablo Bridge crossing an absent Arlanzón River in the ancient city of Burgos.

ford' but the river has been bridged since at least Roman times. Capital of the Rioja region, Logroño's church architecture is a sign of its importance as a stop on the Camino. Today its economy relies heavily on the wines of La Rioja. West of the Ebro the Camino climbs gradually towards the border between La Rioja and Castile & León. Here, tiny Villafranca Montes de Oca was an important bishopric from the third to the eighth century until Arab invaders destroyed it.

The bishopric was eventually relocated to nearby Burgos, which is an enjoyable 30-km downhill ride from the village. Burgos is another waymark for pilgrims, who cross the river Arlanzón here. Often at the forefront of successive conquests, Burgos has been occupied by Celtic, Roman, Visigoth and Berber cultures in its long history. Its surviving fortifications illustrate why the region became known as Castile, the land of castles.

The section between Burgos and León, the next pilgrim city on the Way, is a level ride across the Iberian Central Plateau. León's splendid cathedral, in an airy Gothic style, is known as the House of Light. Nearby, the Casa Botines, a neo-Gothic building by celebrated Barcelona architect Antoni Gaudí, is worth seeing. Crossing the Bernesga river in León, the Camino de Santiago climbs to Astorga, where the episcopal palace is another fine building by Gaudí. The town has well-preserved Roman baths and sewers and, for those with different interests, a Museum of Chocolate.

The route now descends from the plateau to the second largest city in the region of León, Ponferrada. Its twelfth-century Templar castle is a dramatic sight beside the river in the heart of the town. Here another bridge was built for pilgrims, to cross the river Sil. Its reinforcement with iron straps in the eleventh century gave rise to the city's name – literally 'the ironclad bridge'. Iron and coal mining were, until the late twentieth century, the source of the city's wealth. Now the

rising popularity of the Camino de Santiago as a leisure activity is restoring its fortunes, and the Sil valley has several good cycling trails.

West of Ponferrada the route passes through Villafranca del Bierzo, typical of many towns which owe their origins to the Camino de Santiago. It is a crossing point on the river Burbia and soon hostels sprang up to cater for the French pilgrims passing through. There are two monasteries and two twelfth-century churches in Villafranca del Bierzo. Villafranca here and

ABOVE: The New Cathedral at Salamanca was built between 1513 and 1733. They weren't in a rush.

RIGHT: The Episcopal Palace of Astorga by the celebrated Catalan architect Antoni Gaudí, built between 1889 and 1913.

elsewhere on the route means 'French town' or 'town on the French Way'.

From here the Camino inclines sharply to cross from León to Galicia over the Alto de San Roque. Near the summit is the Albergue Linar do Rei, a typical pilgrims' hostel with dormitory sleeping and refectory-style eating, within arched walls and beneath a working bell tower. Next door is more modern accommodation, and between the two this is a popular stop for cyclists who have conquered the climb.

Others prefer to relax at the bottom of the descent from here in Triacastela, a village where the three castles which gave it its name were destroyed by marauding Vikings in the tenth century. A short haul from here the route crosses into the Sarria valley. The town of Sarria is a capsule of Camino features – cloisters, a convent established by wandering Italian monks, a Romanesque bridge and a handsome ruined castle. Beyond Sarria, Portomarín is an unusual village. Its principal buildings were moved brick by brick to their present location when the original village was flooded by the damming of the Minho river in the area. When water is low in the Belesar reservoir you can still see the remains of the old village, its waterfront, and the bridge which made it a part of the Camino.

This is the last major river crossing on the Way and there are less than 100 km to go. At Furelos outside Meride there is a particularly pretty pilgrim footbridge, and from Meride onwards the route makes its descent in gentle stages to Santiago de Compostela itself. Completion of any of the routes to the sacred city is a tremendous achievement for anyone. Imagine how it must have felt for a medieval pilgrim to arrive in the Praza da Quintana in Santiago after the dangers and privations of the road.

All the major Caminos de Santiago are well signposted throughout, with a distinctive logo,

yellow on blue, which could symbolize the various trails converging on Santiago, or the rays of holy light emitting from the city. In fact, it represents the scallop shell which is the sign traditionally carried by pilgrims. You'll see it carved everywhere on churches and hostels along the Way, a reference to the legend which says that St James' body was washed ashore from the sea, undamaged but covered in shells. You may feel entitled to celebrate your own preservation when you dismount in front of the glorious cathedral at your journey's end.

RIGHT: A view of Ponferrada from the castle walls.

BELOW: The town of Villafranca del Bierzo reached by a bridge across the Saint James Burbia river.

BELOW: A sight for sore legs – the conclusion of your pilgrimage ends in the Plaza del Obradoiro.

RIGHT: In the foreground are the remnants of the old Roman Bridge on the Minho river, with its successors beyond.

FAR RIGHT: What the journey has been all about, a chance to be inspired by the interior of the Cathedral of the Apostle at Santiago de Compostela.

The Carretera Austral

Chile

Length: 1,221 km, 759 miles
Start: Puerto Montt
Finish: Villa O'Higgins
Highlights: Ferries at La Arena and Hornopirén, Huequi and Chaitén volcanoes, Puyuhuapi Harbour, El Cóndor Waterfall, Cerro Castillo lagoon, glacier and peak, Bosque Muerto, Marble Caves, Lago Leones

Dense forest, mountains, fjords and glaciers: in Chile the Carretera Austral runs north to south through many ecozones and across several large bodies of water. This is the holiday of a lifetime for the adventurous cyclist.

Chile's Highway 7 was one of the country's biggest infrastructure projects of the twentieth century, aimed at connecting some of the remote communities of the south to the rest of the Chilean road network. Begun in 1976, it was built by 10,000 soldiers of the Chilean Army on the orders of General Pinochet. It also had a key defensive role: before its construction the only surface access to the south was via Argentina, a sometimes hostile neighbour.

Travelling the whole length of the Carretera involves two short ferry journeys and a third one of five hours' duration. You and your bicycle can get to the starting point at Puerto Montt by air and bus. At the other end, travel between O'Higgins and Argentina is complicated but possible by ferry and on foot. Many return to Puerto Montt by a succession of bus services.

Puerto Montt is a port city on the shores of Reloncaví Sound, a sheltered harbour protected by the islands of the Golfo de Ancud. It is the capital of Chile's lake district, Los Lagos, and the city is a fascinating mixture of modern South America and old Germany: it was founded in 1853 by the first of three waves of German colonization of the continent.

Highway 7 follows the shore of the Sound clockwise, crossing the mouth of the Río Coihuin o Chamiza by bridge and the wide Reloncaví Fjord by frequent ferry between La Arena and Puelche. At the village of Contao the road heads inland and skirts the foothills of the Apagado Volcano. Apagado means 'extinct' in Spanish, and the last eruption was in 590 BC.

At Hornopirén the twin rivers Blanco and Negro, 'White' and 'Black', both flow into the Sound. This section of the Carretera is not yet complete; instead, a five-hour ferry voyage charts a course through the narrow waters between steep mainland and densely wooded islands, landing at Leptepu. From here, a short ride across the neck of the volcanic Huequi peninsula leads to the ramp for the short ferry to Caleta Gonzalo. Huequi last erupted only a hundred years ago and was seen smoking in the 1950s.

BELOW LEFT: A loaded car ferry from Hornopirén to Leptepu chugs up Comau Fjord.

BELOW: The route crosses the Río Yelcho south of Chaitén.

OPPOSITE: Los Glaciares National Park.

Much of the land around here is a privately owned conservation park belonging to American philanthropist Douglas Tompkins. He bought it up in 1991 in an effort to save the unspoilt rainforest within it. There's an information centre at Caleta Gonzalo, camping grounds at Lago Río Blanco and some welcome resources in the small harbour town of Chaitén. Chaitén's volcano last erupted in 2011 and its cone is clearly visible from the edge of town looking up the Río Chaitén.

From Chaitén the road cuts inland to the long, fjord-like Lake Yelcho, where in 2017 a deadly landslide closed the Carretera Austral for several months. From its shore the route climbs up and over La Pera Pass, descending with the wide

LEFT: The village of Puerto Gaviota in the temperate rainforest near Isla Magdalena.

BELOW LEFT: There is a short, 0.3km hiking track that will take you to El Cóndor waterfall.

BELOW: The Carretera Austral becomes a gravel track through Cisnes in Aysen Province.

valley of the Río Frío, 'Cold River'. It joins the Río Palena, and at the village of La Junta a fine suspension bridge carries the road over the Río Rosselot at the point where it too joins the Palena. There are restaurants, a minimarket, an airstrip and hotels in La Junta. The road leaves the Palena valley here but soon joins another of its tributaries, the Risopatron, following it upstream to its source, the long, narrow Lago Risopatron. A rollercoaster descent takes you down to the

RIGHT: The Exequiel Gonzáles Bridge over the Río Palena.

BELOW: Cyclists need to be prepared for extended periods of ascending along the route.

coast again and the small town of Puyuhuapi, another former German colony. It has an idyllic harbour at the head of a long fjord and lies in the centre of a cluster of ancient volcanoes. On a still day the reflection of the mountains in the water is quite magical.

This is the last time the Carretera Austral touches the coast until just before its southern end. At the end of the fjord it turns inland up the Queulat river and the many hairpin bends of the Queulat Pass, one of the toughest few kilometres of the

whole trail. On the way down, the road passes the high El Cóndor Waterfall and then follows the long, narrow valley floor of the Cisnes river upstream. A short ladder of hairpin bends climbs away from the river, crossing to Villa Amengual in the wide valley of the Río Travieso. Although the country is still heavily wooded here, you'll notice that the trees are of more temperate species. The mountain tops are bare and there may be traces of snow even in the summer months. The highway squeezes along the eastern shore of Laguna de las Torres at the base of towering

cliffs, then descends with the Río Maniguales to a junction – straight on to Coyhaique (60 km on the unsurfaced Highway 7), or right to Puerto Aysén and Coyhaique (70 km). The latter is paved all the way to Coyhaique and definitely worth the extra 10 km of pedalling.

Coyhaique is the only major settlement on the Carretera Austral apart from Puerto Montt, so

ABOVE: A change of surface as the Carretera Austral follows Route 7 outside Villa Cerro Castillo.

make the most of it. It's a low-lying town on a grid plan, except for the central pentagonal square which reflects the shape of the badge of the police officer who founded the town in 1929. There are a couple of border crossings into Argentina near here. South of Coyhaique the road continues to climb gently in the upper valley of the Simpson, a river popular with anglers. The highest point on the Carretera comes after the road turns away from the valley at El Blanco, but cyclists have already done most of the climbing since Puyuhuapi and can now just enjoy the views. The descent from the Castillo Pass, beneath the jagged peak of Cerro Castillo, is on sharp hairpin bends to Villa Cerro Castillo on the Río Ibáñez. There's a popular day-hike from here to the bluest lagoon you've ever seen, with views of a glacier and Cerro Castillo.

Now the road climbs briefly away from the river to pass beautiful Lago Verde, 'Green Lake', which even on a dull day has a luminous quality about it. As the route drops back down to the Ibáñez

you can see the river's chaotic braided path across the valley floor, and the eerie Bosque Muerto, a forest of dead tree trunks in the middle of the valley.

Now the road leaves the Ibáñez and joins the Murta as it tumbles down to General Carrera Lake, a huge body of water patrolled by the Chilean Navy – the eastern end of it lies in Argentina. At Puerto Río Tranquilo it's worth taking a boat trip or hiring a kayak to visit the Marble Cathedral, a spectacular set of caves at water level and below.

To the west of the route lies the vast Northern Patagonian Ice Field. The Carretera leaves the lake at Puerto Bertrand and follows the River Baker gently downstream to Cochrane. The river carves deep gorges from which the road keeps its distance. This far south and at such an altitude the vegetation is scrubby at best. Plans to dam the Baker were abandoned in 2014 in the face of international environmental objections; few

rivers in the world this long and large remain free and undammed.

Stock up in Cochrane. From here on, the way is even emptier of communities than before. The road flits from valley to valley, with the occasional challenging gradient, before ending abruptly at Puerto Yungay, at sea level on the fjord through which the Río Bravo flows to the Pacific Ocean. With no other option, the ferry across the fjord is free – but only runs twice a day.

ABOVE LEFT: The water-sculpted 'vaults' and 'buttresses' of Patagonia's Marble Cathedral.

TOP: The Bosque Muerto, a forest of dead trees alongside the Río Ibáñez, killed by the eruption of the Hudson volcano.

ABOVE: The route clings to the hillside at Puerto Río Tranquilo.

Now you're on the last leg of the journey, just 102 km to go. This final section of Highway 7 was only completed in 2000 and it's nothing but gravel, with occasional crude embankments across boggy areas and dynamited cuttings through rocky ones. The Carretera follows the Río Bravo, sometimes tucking in on the valley floor under the cliffs, sometimes zig-zagging steeply to get over them.

At the marshy Lagunas del Colorado the highway peels away from the Bravo across the high-altitude plain. It follows the shores of Lake Vargas and the twin-armed Lake Cisnes, and finally picks up the Río Mayer – more evidence of German settlement in that name – and at last seeing the welcoming lights of Villa O'Higgins.

Bernardo O'Higgins is a Chilean national hero, a revolutionary of Spanish and Irish parentage who liberated the country from Spanish rule in 1818. The town named in his honour has accommodation, shops and an airstrip. West of O'Higgins lies the Southern Patagonian Ice Field; to the south, the eight-armed Lago O'Higgins, with O'Higgins Glacier at the end of one of them. The official end of Highway 7 is a few kilometres further on at Puerto Bahamondes, from which a ferry leaves a few times a week to Candelario Mancilla near the Argentinian border. There are plans to extend the Carretera further south, but for now, if you have any energy left, a wooden staircase leads up the hillside to a viewpoint from which you can look over the whole town and some of the magnificent Patagonian wilderness through which you have travelled.

This is a popular ride, particularly among South Americans, and the infrastructure to support it is expanding all the time. But the areas through which it passes are sparsely populated and Highway 7 is not yet fully surfaced. Camping is a practical option for accommodation, but there are also plenty of hostels, guest houses and hotels. You'll get Wi-Fi or cellphone coverage in most towns and villages, but ATMs are still rare. Be prepared with cash, spare parts and two or three days' food supplies; and don't expect to stick to any planned schedule of progress. This is not a trip to be completed with the accuracy of a Japanese railway timetable.

FAR LEFT: Looking down on the confluence between Río Baker and Río Chacabuco.

ABOVE LEFT: The Carretera near Cochrane.

LEFT: Just like taking a bus; the ferry disgorging vehicles at Puerto Yungay.

ABOVE: Counting down the final kilometres as the route approaches Villa O'Higgins.

RIGHT: Villa O'Higgins has two pretty churches side by side, although the majority of completists on the Carretera seek a different kind of spiritual celebration.

Crater Lake Loop

Oregon, USA

Length: 33 miles, 53 km
Start/Finish: Crater Lake Lodge
Highlights: Views in every direction

Mount Mazama in the Cascade Mountains erupted 7,700 years ago and blew itself to smithereens. All that remains is the near-perfect circle of Crater Lake. And if a thing is circular, sooner or later some cyclist is going to want to cycle around it.

Crater Lake National Park is the fifth oldest national park in the USA and the only one in Oregon. At its heart is Crater Lake, five miles wide in diameter, and formed from the flooded remains of an erupted volcanic caldera. As a measure of the intensity of the explosion, not only was Mount Mazama completely destroyed, the crater it created, now filled with water, is 1,949 ft (594 metres) deep, virtually the height of another mountain. It's the deepest lake in the US and the ninth deepest in the world.

Filled only by direct rain and snowfall, the water is a remarkable shade of deep blue. No streams flow into or out of it. It is completely encircled by the steep, jagged remains of Mount Mazama, which varies in height between 1,000 and 2,000 ft (305 and 610 metres) above the lake's surface. A visitor centre sits on top of the rim at the south-western corner of the lake, and a scenic circuit has been engineered around the rim.

Like any scenic route along the side of a mountain range, it has its ups and downs. Although it's only 33 miles in length, there's enough for you not to wish it were longer, nor so much hard work that you wish it were shorter. In total there are 3,035 ft (925 metres) of ascents.

There is parking at the visitor centre complex and the busy Crater Lake Lodge, and most cyclists ride in a clockwise direction. This means the busiest stretch of the loop, on a through road with more traffic, is quickly completed; travelling clockwise also puts the cyclist on the lakeward side of the road, enabling the most photogenic views across the water from the ridge-top parts of the ride. And towards the southern end, the loop drops down below the level of the lake, providing an enjoyable and dynamic climb at the ride's end.

It's best to start the ride early in the day before the motorists arrive. If you're especially worried about sharing the route with cars, visit on the third weekend in September, when the park authorities close all but the eight-mile through section of the road to vehicles. Whenever you come, bear in mind that parts of the road are up to 8,000 ft (2,438 metres) above sea level. It's cool even in the summer, and snow can linger on the slopes of the crater as late as August. The scenic road is closed in winter, when hardy souls have been known to use it as a cross-country skiing circuit.

This really is the perfect day ride, hard enough to provide a workout but through a geologically and botanically remarkable landscape where every climb, every descent, every twist and turn opens up new and uplifting views.

TOP: A view of West Rim Drive and Hillman Peak.

ABOVE: The western entrance to Crater Lake National Park.

OPPOSITE: A spectacular morning cloud pattern develops over Wizard Island and the caldera rim.

The River Danube

Austria

Length: 325 km, 202 miles
Start: Passau
Finish: Vienna
Highlights: Schlögen View, Linzer torte, Schloss Greinburg, Grein Theatre, Melk Abbey, castles of Aggstein, Hinterhaus and Dürnstein, apricot brandy from Krems, Göttweig Abbey, everything about Vienna, Sacher torte

Freight barges and cruise ships ply the waters of the mighty Danube. But the best way to see the river, and the life and scenery that surrounds it, is at the leisurely pace of a bicycle holiday. The ride through Austria is an easy week's cycling.

The Danube trail is known as the Route of Emperors and Kings because of its role throughout millennia of history. The river is the second-longest in Europe after the Volga, with a length of 2,850 km (1,170 miles) from start to finish. All but about 450 km of it are navigable, and it has been a crucial trade route for thousands of years. It has been a natural border of dynasties and kingdoms since Celtic times, and the sprawling Austro-Hungarian Empire was assembled on either side of its banks. Today it flows through four national capitals – Vienna, Bratislava, Budapest and Belgrade – and still forms a boundary between Slovakia and Hungary, Croatia and Serbia, Serbia and Romania, and Romania and Bulgaria.

It is possible to cycle the whole length of the River Danube from its source in Germany's Black Forest to its delta on the Black Sea in Romania, although it might take you a couple of months. The section between Passau and Vienna is by far the most popular, and several tour companies offer support packages of accommodation and luggage

conveyance. The difference in altitude between Passau and Vienna is so little that you won't even notice you're going downhill – about 300 metres (984 ft) in the course of the 325-km route.

The route starts in Passau, just over the border in Germany. It's a busy town where almost a quarter of the population are students at Passau University. It's a good place to make sure your bike is in top condition for the road ahead. It stands at the confluence of three rivers: the Danube, the Inn, which forms the border between Austria and Germany, and the Ilz, which feeds in water from southern Bavaria. Many river cruises start from Passau and it's best to start cycling from here too – the great majority of the 38,000 cyclists who ride this trail do so, so you won't be riding against the flow of traffic as well as the river.

East of Passau the Danube takes over border duties from the Inn (which another route in this book follows) for the next 27 km, between steep wooded mountainsides at whose bases there is barely enough flat ground for the occasional small village. At Schlögen the river starts a series of bends so tight that, with a short walk uphill to a vantage point, you can gaze a considerable distance both upstream and down at the same time.

Many villages have landing stages for the Donaubus, a bus service on water. Some, like

OPPOSITE: Colours collide at the meeting of three rivers in Passau: the Danube, Inn and Ilz.

TOP: The Schlögener loop of the Danube near Schlögen.

ABOVE RIGHT: A river walk near the Lentos Art Museum, Linz.

RIGHT: Greinburg Castle at Grein an der Donau.

Ottensheim, have been traditional ferry ports across the river. Although Ottensheim ferry still runs, most vehicle crossings have been replaced by bridges. Linz, the largest city between Passau and Vienna, has three bridges, all built since World War II when their predecessors were bombed during attacks on the city's oil refinery.

Hitler lived here as a young boy and preferred Linz to Vienna. He intended to make Linz the cultural capital of the Third Reich after the war and constructed large industrial areas on the banks of the Danube to boost the city's economy. Linz was the first Austrian city to confront its Nazi past after the war, and downstream at

Mauthausen there is a memorial to victims of the concentration camp there. Today Linz is a rail hub, a university town, and a thriving financial and commercial centre with an international airport – the nearest to Passau if you're flying in to follow this trail. Linz is world famous for its Linzer torte, a tart of fruit and nuts covered in a lattice of pastry.

The town of Grein further downstream grew up around Schloss Greinburg, a splendid fifteenth-century Germanic castle with a three-tiered courtyard. Grein also boasts Austria's oldest theatre. Further on at Ybbs there is one of several hydro-electric schemes across the Danube,

ABOVE: Melk Abbey contains the tomb of Saint Coloman of Stockerau and the remains of several members of the House of Babenberg, Austria's rulers before the Habsburgs.

which also serves as a bridge between Ybbs and its sister Persenbeug-Gottsdorf on the other side. Persenbeug Castle sits in a commanding position overlooking the river.

So too does Melk Abbey, visible against the skyline from all directions and one of the great sights of any Danube trip. The monastery and centre of learning was founded in the eleventh century but made over in exuberant Gothic style in the early eighteenth. It has survived many threats to its existence from invasion, political

BELOW: Dürnstein Abbey at the water's edge, with the old castle on the hill.

BOTTOM: Steiner Tor, the symbol of the city of Krems an der Donau.

BOTTOM RIGHT: The Neptune Fountain and the Gloriette in the gardens of the Schönbrunn Palace in Vienna.

and religious reform, and on several occasions devastating fires – most recently in 1974.

Between Melk and Krems the Danube valley is known as the Wachau, internationally recognized as the finest wine-growing region of Austria. It's also the setting for three fine, ruined medieval castles perched on rocky outcrops by the river. Aggstein Castle was the stronghold of a robber baron nicknamed Schreckenwald, who preyed on Danube shipping by enforcing expensive tolls on all who passed. Hinterhaus has great views of the river and the Wachau vineyards. Dürnstein is famous as the castle in which Richard the Lionheart, King of England, was imprisoned and held for ransom after the Third Crusade.

Krems is the last major town on the Danube before Vienna. It's a handsome town with an impressive city gate, the Steiner Tor. Its gastronomic reputation hangs on its production of Austria's favourite liqueur, Marillenschnaps – apricot brandy. The town is literally overshadowed by the enormous complex of the Göttweig Abbey on a hill on the opposite bank of the Danube. As much a fortified castle as an abbey, Göttweig has a priceless library.

And finally you arrive in Vienna. It's a great city for cycling, very flat and well served with traffic-free cycling lanes – but watch out for scooters, which (like Paris) are increasingly popular in the city. It would take a whole book to list Vienna's attractions – its art, its music, its Habsburg imperial architecture. It is a monumental capital which manages to be friendly and informal at the same time. Vienna's café culture is unique, and if you do nothing else here, soak up the atmosphere in one of its old coffeehouses with an unhurried coffee and a Sacher torte, and perhaps a small glass of Sekt (Austrian prosecco) to celebrate your arrival.

Dutch Coastal Route

The Netherlands

Length: 570 km, 354 miles
Start: Sluis
Finish: Bad Nieuweschans
Highlights: Sluis, Cornelia Quackshofje, Madurodam, Egmond aan Zee, Afsluitdijk, Harlingen, Uitwierde, Borgsweer

The Netherlands are flat. Even inland the steepest climbs are the ramps to bridges over motorways. A cycling holiday in the country is a leisurely ride through a landscape of sand dunes and forests, pretty villages and towns.

The Nederlandse Kustroute, the Dutch Coastal Route, is part of the much longer North Sea Cycle Route, EuroVelo 12. This section travels the whole length of the Low Countries' hard-won border with the sea. Some bald statistics tell a story of ingenious land reclamation over the centuries. Only 50% of the country stands more than a single metre above sea level; 17% of the country's current area has been reclaimed from lakes or the sea with the construction of dykes, and 26% of that area is below sea level, so the maintenance of dykes is crucial.

The reclaimed land is called polder, and its creation has brought many changes to the local economy. Former fishing villages are now miles from the sea and have turned to dairy farming; former islands are now hills or peninsulas. In the country's most ambitious project, an entire sea – the Zuiderzee inlet – was reclaimed, partly as a non-tidal lake but largely as land. Shipwrecks were exposed. Cornelis Lely was the nineteenth-century designer of the scheme and an entire new city, Lelystad, 'Lely City', now stands where once it would have been under water.

You will see much evidence of this activity on a ride from south to north along the coast. Sluis, the starting point of the Coastal Route, was a

BELOW: A typical coastal panorama near Ouddorp in South Holland.

BELOW LEFT: Cycling alongside the tree-lined Damse Vaart canal (dug on the command of Napoleon) near Sluis.

Belgian port which gave its name to a 1340 sea battle nearby. The area around the town was once four small islands in the estuary of the Scheldt river but now forms its left bank. Today Sluis is some 10 km from the sea, but still has a quay and its old defensive walls.

The coast north of Sluis is popular with Belgian and Dutch beach lovers, as you'll see in places like Cadzand-Bad and Fort Soleil. From the harbour at Breskens a passenger and bicycle ferry takes you across the river to Vlissingen, on the former island of Walcheren. Cars have had their own tunnel since 2003. Vlissingen, 'Flushing' in English, has been an important ship-building port for centuries, often at the forefront of international conflict. There are historical buildings associated with such events – a fort,

the Arsenaal, barracks – and others connected with the sea, including the charming Cornelia Quackshofje, a courtyard of almshouses for the widows and orphans of sailors, built in 1643 and still in use.

North of Vlissingen the road hugs the coast as it hops from island to island, among them the artificial island of Neeltje Jans, built to aid the

construction of one of the dams on which the road is carried. After Ouddorp the route finds its way through the vast dock complex of Europort, where a ferry will carry you across the mouth of the river Maas to the Hook of Holland – the hook-shaped point of land is much less obvious now that so much land has been reclaimed on the opposite shore. The Maas (called the Meuse in its French reaches) is one of several rivers, including the mighty Rhine, which come together in the area to form a complicated delta. The waterways here still carry goods to and from the heart of Europe.

The Hook marks the southern end of a 75-km-long straight stretch of sandy beach. Inland there may be towns and villages but they are hidden from sight behind sand dunes. Apart from occasional beach huts and bars, there is little evidence that the Netherlands' three largest cities – Rotterdam, Den Haag (The Hague) and Amsterdam – lie just out of sight.

It's easy cycling. With flatness however comes a lack of shelter from winds across the North Sea or through the English Channel from the Atlantic. It is no wonder that since 2018 the Dutch railway network has run entirely on wind-generated electricity. For cyclists, a following wind can be a blessing, but an unremitting headwind is a distinct handicap to both speed and pleasure.

Only in one place does urban life break through the dunes, at Scheveningen, the port next to The Hague. Soon after Naaktstrand Kijduin, a nudist beach, the Dutch Coastal Route swings inland to avoid the busy harbour, unfortunately bypassing Scheveningen's magnificent leisure pier built in 1959 to replace one destroyed during World War II. Instead, as if by compensation, the route passes close to Madurodam, a 1:25 scale model city. It occupies a huge area and features recreations of many famous Dutch and international buildings, as well as fully functioning railways, motorways, airport and

shipping lanes. If you are travelling with children (large or small), allow plenty of time.

Madurodam lies between Scheveningen and The Hague, the administrative centre of the country and home to several important international courts. It's a city with a long and proud history, and beautiful buildings to match, nestled in the shade of a towering modern skyline. Beyond it the route returns to the shore as far as Zandvoort, where it swings east into the National Park of Zuid-Kennemerland, ancient woodland growing on even older sand dunes. It's criss-crossed by paths and popular with locals from the beautiful city of Haarlem to the east. At Haarlem's heart is a magnificent old square and cathedral. The city was a centre of gold and silver work and the cathedral is still surrounded by their workshops and outlets. Although Amsterdam is not on the coast, it is only a short bike ride from Haarlem to the Dutch capital with its canals, galleries and night life.

The route emerges from the dunes into the outskirts of IJmuiden, the ferry terminal for passengers to and from northern Britain. A small vehicle ferry makes the short crossing of Amsterdam's busy river, the Amstel.

North of the river the route continues in parallel with another 75-km stretch of sandy coastline, sometimes drifting inland to weave through the dunes. If you venture a little further still, to the east, you'll see rich farming country, acres of tulips in season and fields of livestock for the important Dutch dairy industry, all punctuated by small towns and villages of enormous character. On the coast, Egmond aan Zee is worth a visit. Founded in AD 977, it has fought a losing battle with the sea. As much of it lies *beneath* the waves

LEFT: A view of Vlissingen from the Arsenaal Tower.

OPPOSITE: Scheveningen beach is the most popular stretch of sand in Holland.

as beside them. In the late nineteenth century it was something of an artists' colony, led by the American painters George Hitchcock, Walter MacEwen, and Gari Melchers who settled there. This stretch of the route is on the western arm of the former Zuiderzee, a 100-km tidal inlet of the North Sea which used to be Amsterdam's main access to open water. In 1932 a 32-km dam across it, the Afsluitdijk ('closing-off dyke'), was completed, blocking it off from saltwater. It is a twentieth-century marvel, stretching from Den Oever in the province of North Holland to Zurich in Friesland. Behind it sits the resulting freshwater lake the IJsselmeer, much smaller than the Zuiderzee thanks to the reclamation of two huge polders made possible by the dam.

There is literally and metaphorically a lot of pressure on the Afsluitdijk – it would be a humanitarian disaster if it broke and flooded the land it now defends. Reinforcement work is currently being undertaken, forcing the periodic closure of bicycle lanes. A replacement bus service carries bikes and their riders across instead. Friesland is one of the most rural of Dutch provinces, far from the busy cities further south. As you ride this last leg of the route, look out for terps – small hills on which villages were built to keep out of the reach of rising waters.

The coastal trail passes through the charming town of Harlingen, whose quays are lined with typical old Dutch sailing vessels and merchants' houses. Ferries from here serve the arc of small islands just offshore. As the route turns east along the northern coast of the Netherlands it encounters the scene of another battle between man and nature. In 1280 a terrible tidal flood engulfed the mouth of the river Lauwers, forming a new bay called the Lauwerszee. Nearly 700

TOP: The reward for tackling the Dutch Coastal Route in spring is field upon field of tulips.

LEFT: There isn't a tremendous amount of local interest on the Afsluitdijk, but if you're a big fan of seabirds and crosswinds…

years later in 1953, and again in 1954, tidal surges and heavy rain again caused disastrous damage and loss of life. In one of the most recent acts of reclamation, a dam across the inlet was completed in 1969, reclaiming the lost area of land. The Coastal Route crosses this barrier. As with the Zuiderzee, a new freshwater lake, the Lauwersmeer, has been created and now forms part of a national nature reserve.

The final few kilometres of the Coastal Route offer contrast between the old and the new. Delfzijl has been the Netherlands' most important northern port for centuries and is a bustling modern town with much of its past on display. The church at nearby Uitwierde is interesting because it is built on an ancient artificial mound to raise it above flood levels. A stone tomb dating from 3400 BC has been discovered in the area. To the east of Delfzijl, the unspoilt villages of Borgsweer and Termunten are glimpses of a pre-industrial age.

The Dutch Coastal Route ends in the small town of Bad Nieuweschans. Nieuweschans means 'new fortifications', and the town's defensive walls (of which a section of the moat remains today) were built in the seventeenth century when the Netherlands, Belgium and Luxemburg rose up against their Spanish rulers. The result was a partial success, leading to the formation of a Dutch Republic in the north of the present country while Spain retained its southern Dutch provinces. The prefix Bad was added to the town's name in 2009 to promote it as a spa destination. After 570 km, this may be exactly what you are looking for.

ABOVE: Zuiderhaven harbour at Harlingen has a fine collection of classic Dutch vessels mixed in with the commercial fishing fleet.

RIGHT: The Old Reformed Church in Uitwierde, Groningen.

Elbe Cycle Path

Czechia/Germany

Length: 211 km, 131 miles
Start: Prague
Finish: Dresden
Highlights: Prague Castle and Charles Bridge, Veltrusy Mansion, Mělník Castle, Litoměřice, Elbe Sandstone Mountains, Střekov Castle, Děčín (castle, riverside and synagogue), Fortress Königstein, Miniature Saxon Switzerland, Dresden Frauenkirche

Name a European riverside bicycle trail and most people will name the Loire and the Danube. But the lesser known Elbe has been voted the favourite river route of German cyclists for thirteen straight years. What's its secret?

The Elbe rises in the Giant Mountains on the Czech-Polish border and at first flows south before turning west towards Prague, and then north-west through Dresden, Magdeburg and Hamburg into the North Sea at Cuxhaven. This indirect route from source to sea makes the Elbe's catchment area the fourth largest in Europe, and around 25 million people live in the Elbe basin, depending on the water that the river and its tributaries provide.

The Elbe Cycle Path officially starts in Špindlerův Mlýn, a Czech snowsport centre in the Giant Mountains with many MTB trails open during the summer. From there it runs the entire length of the river, about 1,220 km. It does not, however, pass through the Czech capital, Prague, which sits on the Vltava river. The Vltava joins the Elbe about 35 km north of the city, and the most popular section of the Elbe Cycle Path is a route from Prague to Dresden using both rivers.

The trail is very flat and very well signposted – in Czechia it follows National Routes 7 and 2, and in Germany it's Route D10. It passes through historic riverside towns and dramatic natural scenery, with reminders of life before the Iron Curtain rose and fell. The entire route runs through the former Eastern Bloc countries of Czechoslovakia and East Germany.

Prague is a noble city with a long history, and worth spending a day or two in before you set off. Prague's tenth-century castle towers above the city and its university is named after Charles IV, Holy Roman Emperor at the time of its founding in 1348. It is the oldest such institution in Central Europe. The statue-lined Charles Bridge over the Vltava, begun in 1357, also bears his name. More recently Prague has earned a reputation for its night life and (to a lesser extent) its tradition of puppet theatre.

The Vltava leaves the city heading north through the outskirts. The cycle path follows the right bank, soon passing the estate of the Baroque Veltrusy Mansion. Veltrusy was originally built in the eighteenth century for Count Václav Antonín Chotek of Chotkov and Vojnín. You may glimpse stately pavilions in its grounds dedicated to the

TOP: EuroVelo 7 passes the Veltrusy château that stands near the Vltava River.

ABOVE RIGHT: The Elbe and two branches of the Vltava meet at Mělník.

RIGHT: Looking back from the river at Mělník Castle.

OPPOSITE: A rock arch in the Elbe Sandstone Mountains, this one in Swiss Bohemia.

Habsburg empress Maria Theresa and others, evidence of Czechia's royalist, pre-communist past.

Beyond the Veltrusy Mansion the Vltava turns east through open countryside to join the Elbe at Mělník. Early coins prove that Mělník was already an important centre in the eleventh century and its castle and church date from that time. Today, the town centre has a colourful feel, and the castle, confiscated by the state under communism, has been returned to its previous owner, Prince Lobkowicz. The route continues now on the left bank of the Elbe (called the Labe in Czech) as far as Roudnice nad Labem (Roudnice on the Elbe). The Elbe Path crosses the river here and continues to Litoměřice, a wine-growing town with around three kilometres of underground cellars built on three levels, some of which are open to the public.

The countryside along this stretch is known as the Garden of Bohemia and its warm climate appeals to fruit growers and retired citizens alike. Historically part of German-speaking Bohemia, the area became part of newly created Czechoslovakia after World War I. Germans knew it as the Sudetenland, and Hitler reclaimed Litoměřice and its surroundings in 1938. Czech resistance fighters backed by the Red Army retook the town in 1945, and in the aftermath of World War II, all Germans (even those with long family histories in the lands of Czechoslovakia) were expelled from the country.

The Elbe continues northwards into Bohemian Switzerland – not the country but a range of sandstone mountains, which rain and the river have eroded into remarkable cliffs and towers of rock. This is the scenic highlight of the route as the path runs along the base of the cliffs for some 15 km.

LEFT: Two cyclists on EuroVelo 7 cycling towards Střekov Castle in the Czech Republic.

It emerges under the romantic ruins of fourteenth-century Střekov Castle which, like Mělník Castle, was returned to the princely Lobkowicz family after the fall of communism. Richard Wagner's opera *Tannhäuser* was inspired by its setting, and the poet Goethe thought the view from it the most beautiful in Europe.

Střekov guards the river approach to the large industrial city Ústí nad Labem. East of Ústí lies beautiful Děčín with its dramatic royal castle and colourful nineteenth-century riverside buildings. Chopin wrote waltzes here, and Děčín Synagogue is an Art Nouveau masterpiece. Just downstream from Děčín the walls of the valley close in again around Elbe Canyon, where buildings have their backs to the cliffs. At an unassuming row of bollards across the cycle path you enter Germany – the border is the Klopotský Potok, a small stream that enters the Elbe here, and it's worth walking a few hundred metres to the Klopotský Waterfall, which tumbles into a rock-walled swimming pool.

Above the town of Königstein stretches the vast Fortress Königstein, one of the largest hilltop castles in Europe. Known as the Saxon Bastille, it has never been captured, and served as a forbidding prison for much of its life. During World War II only one man, a French general, managed to escape. A little further on, above the village of Stadt Wehlen, is Miniature Saxon Switzerland, a landscaped park of tiny mountains and buildings including the fortress, with working model trains, planes and boats.

Now, as the houses and river traffic multiply, the Elbe flows gracefully to the conclusion of this route in Dresden. Dresden's elegant renaissance appearance today is a miracle of reconstruction after the bombing of the city during World War II by British and American air forces. The city, the former royal capital of Saxony, benefited greatly from the reunification of Germany in 1990. Its economy is booming and its population is getting younger. The symbolic 2005 restoration of the damaged Frauenkirche, left as a battered shell for 50 years as a reminder of the folly of war, reflects the city's rebirth. If your own shell is feeling a little battered after your trip along the Elbe, you too can find restoration in Dresden.

ABOVE LEFT: No tough climbs on this part of the route near Děčín in the Czech Republic.

TOP: A hilltop restaurant-with-a-view at Děčín.

MIDDLE: Another place to get a spectacular view of the river is from the castle at Königstein in the Saxon Swiss National Park.

BOTTOM: The historic Dresden waterfront is a popular stopping-off point for river cruises.

L'Eroica

Italy

Length: 209 km, 130 miles
Start/Finish: Gaiole in Chianti, Tuscany
Highlights: Gaiole, Castiglion del Bosco,
Montalcino, Radda in Chianti

The route began life as an event which celebrated the noble Italian history of the sport of cycling. Participants are encouraged to wear vintage clothing and ride vintage bicycles over unpaved country roads. No wonder its founder chose the name L'Eroica: 'The Heroic One'.

Giancarlo Brocci is the man who founded L'Eroica. Growing up in the region of Chianti in Tuscany, Brocci never went to school because his communist parents didn't want him to be taught by nuns. Instead, he spent his days at the local bar, reading the newspapers to old men who had never learned to read for themselves.

The sports pages were full of the bitter rivalry of the day between road racers Gino Bartali and Fausto Coppi – the former a traditionalist admired in the rural south of the country, the latter an innovator in diet and training revered in the industrial north. Italians are as passionate about cycling as they are about football, or any other sport; Brocci was caught up in the epic duals between the two men during the 1940s and 1950s, in what the Italians still see as the Golden Age of cycling in their country.

As an adult Brocci became involved in politics and the environment. He campaigned to make Chianti a destination for cycling tourism. In 1995 he created the Gran Fondo Gino Bartali, 'Big Ride', in honour of his hero. The endurance

race caught the imagination of the sport and attracted more entrants every year. Recognizing the nation's nostalgia for the Golden Age, he introduced L'Eroica in 1997. Bartali, then still alive, had retired from racing in 1960, the same year as Coppi's death.

RIGHT AND BELOW: Classic Tuscan vistas are constantly unfolding, as you cycle the white roads of Chianti.

Anyone may ride in L'Eroica. It's not a race but a participatory celebration; as much a festival as a sporting event. Its full name was originally L'Eroica Strade Bianche – 'the heroic race on white roads' – a reference to the dusty unpaved country roads of Tuscany on which much of the ride takes place. These are the roads on which the cycling heroes of the past trained and raced; entrants in L'Eroica are encouraged to ride in old-fashioned cycling gear and to ride vintage bicycles.

The term has strict parameters. A vintage bicycle should have a steel frame with external brake and gear cables; gear levers should be mounted on the down tube, not on the handlebars; if desired, the pedals should have toe straps, not cleats; and each wheel should be of traditional shallow profile, with at least 32 spokes. You may ride a modern bike in modern lycra sportswear, but only the full vintage will earn you a certificate of completion.

The route is signposted and open to anyone all year round. It starts and finishes in Gaiole, a scattered village between Siena and Florence which was named by Forbes as Europe's most idyllic place to live. The arrival of hundreds of cyclists on the first Sunday in October, when the event is run, may briefly shatter that idyll. Riders start early: faster riders at 5am, slower ones at 7am. Stragglers may return long after dark: that is, those who intend to finish the course in a single day.

L'Eroica plots a figure-of-eight course across the rolling hills of Tuscany, and a third of the route is still on unmade vineyard and farm tracks. It climbs over 3,800 metres (12,467 ft) in total, and although much of that is due to the gentle rise and fall of the landscape, there are four major ascents – two of them in the last 30 km

RIGHT: Starting out in Gaiole, think carefully about your adhesive before applying a false moustache for 209 km.

of the route. The first, 5 km south of Gaiole and 5 km long, climbs 200 metres (656 ft) through vineyards to the village of La Madonna where it transfers to the first of fifteen stretches of the celebrated 'white roads'.

Dropping down to cross the river Arbia at Pianella, L'Eroica makes its way south-west to the outskirts

of Siena before heading south again through poplar-lined avenues with glorious views across the province. Shortly before Castiglion del Bosco, 'the castle in the woods', the hills rise again and L'Eroica begins its second major incline, a rise of almost 500 metres (1,640 ft) over only 14 km. You may want to pause to admire the recently restored castle and the produce of its excellent vineyards.

The descent from the summit at Poggio del Tagliatone is thrilling and almost as steep as the climb, passing through the handsome hilltop town of Montalcino as L'Eroica turns once again northwards. At Buonconvento (the name means 'happy place') the route briefly follows the valley of the Arbia before veering eastwards into the hills around the peaks of Poggio d'Arno

and Poggio della Fornace. Crossing itself as it traverses the river again at Pianella, L'Eroica begins its third ascent, 270 metres (886 ft) over the 10 km road to Vagliagli, and soon after that its fourth and final climb through the olive groves of Radda in Chianti at the northern end of the route. The last 9 km are all downhill.

L'Eroica has also been, since 2007, the setting for a professional road race, already hailed as a classic, called the Strade Bianche, run annually in March. The original L'Eroica remains not a race but an experience. And it's a popular one. The format has now been adopted by events in three other areas of Italy and in seven other countries around the world: Japan, South Africa, Spain, Germany, the Netherlands, England and California. In Tuscany, which is a photographer's and food lover's paradise, riders are actively encouraged to sample its many pleasures along the way. The fastest riders can complete the route in under nine hours, but why not take a few days over it?

OPPOSITE: Looking across the rooftops of Montalcino in the Val d'Orcia from the town's medieval fort.

ABOVE: Vineyards on the hillside outside Gaiole remind you that you're in the heart of Chianti.

RIGHT: With permanent signing for the route, cyclists can tackle it any time of the year … with modern bikes.

Flanders Beer Routes

Belgium

Length: 28–55 km, 17–34 miles
Start/Finish: Steenhuffel
Highlights: BEER, Diepensteyn Castle, Breendonk Fort, Duvel Moortgat Brewery, Bouchout Castle, Eddy Merckx Bicycle Factory, Grimbergen Castle and Abbey Church, Keersmaeker Brewery

Other countries may be famed for their wines but no one does beer like the Belgians. To prove their love for the stuff, there are eight official beer-themed cycling routes through Flanders. Politely, none of them uses the word 'crawl'.

The Flanders Beer Routes vary in length but each of them is easily achievable in a day, provided you don't linger too long in any of the many breweries and hostelries along the way. They are all designed as loops, but they can be combined to make longer trails.

Flanders is fairly flat, and none of the loops climbs above 150 metres (492 ft). Belgium uses the same system for cycle paths as Holland: every junction is numbered, and at each one signs point you to adjacent junctions, usually with an accompanying map of the immediate area. With the help of a cycling map, you simply note the numbers of the junctions through which you plan to pass. It takes a little getting used to, but it saves a lot of time and head-scratching once you're underway.

Steenhuffel makes a good base and starting point for three of the routes. It has a brewing tradition going back at least 270 years. The earliest reference to the town's De Hoorn brewery is in 1747, and it's now the headquarters of Palm, the company that owns De Hoorn and several other Belgian breweries. Just outside Steenhuffel, the brewery also owns Diepensteyn Castle, a moated brick-built medieval castle (pictured opposite) which it has restored and where it now keeps its hard-working dray horses.

BOTTOM LEFT AND RIGHT: Two images of the Palm Brewery in Steenhuffel.

BELOW: Lest we forget: Fort Breendonk has a pictorial reminder of its wartime occupiers.

69

ABOVE: Imitating Kew's Victorian glasshouses, the National Botanic Garden at Meise.

TOP: The neo-Gothic Bouchout Castle in the grounds of the Botanic Garden.

ABOVE RIGHT: Grimbergen has a fine seventeenth-century watermill that still grinds flour.

In this flat land, moats were a common line of defence, and in nearby Breendonk a huge fort is surrounded by water. It now houses a museum about its grim final use, as a concentration camp during World War II. The fort sits on ground previously occupied by the Romans, who took advantage of its source of fresh water. Today, it is said, the same pure source is used by Breendonk's Duvel Moortgat Brewery. Duvel pale ale is one of the best known of Belgian beers, and the company also owns other famous Belgian brands including Brasserie d'Achouffe,

De Koninck and Liefmans, which makes classic Belgian fruit beers.

Nearby Kapelle-op-den-Bos ('the chapel in the woods') boasts two more modest and recently founded breweries – Chapel Brewery and Den Triest microbrewery. The town is an important transport hub, at a point where the Mechelen–Ghent railway crosses the Willebroek–Brussels canal; and the chapel, the parish church of St Nicolas, was one of the first casualties of heavy bombing by the advancing German army during

World War II. It has been rebuilt with some modern changes.

South of Kapelle-op-den-Bos, Bouchout Castle is a twelfth-century fortification transformed into a seventeenth-century renaissance palace in the style of the Loire, almost completely surrounded by an artificial lake. Its vast landscaped grounds, in the town of Meise, are now a botanical garden with a stunning crown-shaped glasshouse. Of greater interest to cyclists may be the town's Eddy Merckx bicycle factory, named after Belgium's most famous cycling son.

Nearby, the moated and ruined Grimbergen Castle is just one of four in the town of Grimbergen. Grimbergen Beer is now brewed by Carlsberg at several sites around Europe, and no longer in its native town; but its brewing (like most historic alcoholic libations) was originally the work of monks, in this instance twelfth-century Norbertine monks at Grimbergen Abbey. Today all that remains of the abbey is the Baroque Grimbergen parish church with its 49-bell carillon, set in an old square with Grimbergen Beer Museum next door.

Like Grimbergen beer, brands and breweries change hands, sometimes disappearing and sometimes becoming part of a larger concern. The tiny village of Kobbegem has a seventeenth-century brewery still run by the De Keersmaeker family, which now makes beers for the Alken-Maes Belgian brewing company. Alken-Maes were responsible for persuading Grimbergen's monks to allow the commercial development of their beer after World War II. In the Keersmaeker Brewery they now make Mort Subite – 'Sudden Death' – a range of lambic beers fermented with local yeasts and bacteria instead of the more common, specially prepared brewers' yeasts. Lambic beers are something of a Belgian speciality, and Mort Subite is named after a famous café in Brussels where lawyers used to gamble between cases. The hand in play at the

time when they were recalled to the courthouse was ended instantly: a quick win for the best hand, sudden death for the losers.

Beer tourism is very popular in Belgium and every brewery has a visitor centre and tasting café. The trick is to enjoy all that they have to offer without falling off your bicycle, which would be sudden death to the rest of your cycling holiday.

ABOVE AND RIGHT: Three images from the Mort Subite lambic brewery in Kobbegem. Most Belgian beermakers *can* manage to organize a sampling in their brewery.

The Garden Route

South Africa

Length: 300 km, 186 miles
Start: Port Elizabeth
Finish: Cape Town
Highlights: Tsitsikamma Forest, Knysna Lagoon, Kaaimans River railway bridge and grotto, Outeniqua Pass, Cango Caves, Oudtshoorn Ostrich Safari, Mossel Bay, Struisbaai, Cape Agulhas, Betty's Bay penguin colony, whale and shark watching, Klein-Hangklip Mountain, Table Mountain

One of the most beautiful stretches of coastline anywhere on the African continent lies between East Cape on the Indian Ocean and West Cape on the Atlantic. It's a popular drive for motorists, but there's no substitute for cycling the route.

A fit cyclist could ride South Africa's Garden Route in three days. But with so much so see along the way, it makes a gentle and stimulating one- or two-week trip through the sights, sounds and smells of the southern tip of the African continent. Summer in South Africa runs from November to March and the route is at its busiest around the Christmas holidays. The best time to cycle it is in late summer or early autumn – between February and April – or in the spring of September and October when there are good opportunities for whale-watching.

The route sets off from Port Elizabeth and in its early stages passes through the Tsitsikamma Forest, a national park of indigenous species including the keurboom tree with its orchid-like purple flowers. Stretched along 80 km of dramatic coastline the park incorporates the mouths of

the Storms, Tsitsikamma and Keurbooms rivers – Tsitsikamma means 'clear water'.

Keurboomstrand is a relaxed holiday resort with a lively, endless beach along the edge of Plettenberg Bay. The rocky promontory at the southern end of the bay is Robberg Nature Reserve, an area of both land and marine conservation. The zone includes several marine habitats and is visited by many species of shark and turtle. Scuba diving is permitted.

Knysna is a good place to break your journey. It stands on the northern shore of a large lagoon formed by the Knysna River before it breaks through a narrow gap between two headlands into the ocean. The headlands are punctured with sea caves and edged with fine beaches. Boat trips on the lagoon are a popular activity; and just north of the town, Millwood Forest was the scene of South Africa's first gold rush.

West of Knysna a string of lakes leads to the resort town of Wilderness, with handsome beaches and occasional fierce weather. Above Wilderness, a short climb on a gravel track takes you to the Map of Africa Viewpoint: below you,

OPPOSITE: Feel the rush of water at Storms River Mouth in Tsitsikamma National Park.

TOP: Robberg Nature Reserve at Plettenberg Bay.

MIDDLE: The magnificent Kaaimans River railway bridge.

BOTTOM: A landform known as 'The Map of Africa' carved out by the Kaaimans River.

a series of sharp bends and deep gorges in the Kaaimans River form the shape of the African continent. South Africa's last steam railway connected Wilderness with Knysna to the east and George to the west, but services have been suspended since 2009. Instead you can walk the line through a tunnel from Wilderness to a restaurant previously accessible only by train, next to the eccentrically decorated Kaaimans Grotto. Just around the corner is the spectacular Kaaimans River railway viaduct which you can also walk across.

ABOVE: You can learn all about the ostrich trade at the C. P. Nel Museum in Oudtshoorn.

RIGHT: This long and winding road leads to the impressive Outeniqua Pass.

It's possible to stick to the coast west of George, but most versions of the Garden Route take you inland from there to Oudtshoorn over the twisting Outeniqua Pass, from which every hairpin bends offers a better view than the last of the ocean below. About 30 km north of Oudtshoorn lie the Cango Caves, a jaw-dropping series of dripstone caverns. Visitor numbers are limited in this natural wonder, and guided tours must be booked ahead.

Oudtshoorn is the centre of South Africa's ostrich-farming economy, the self-styled Feather Capital of the World. The town thrived during two periods of fashion history during which ostrich feathers were a must-have accessory, the 1860s and the early twentieth century. Ostrich safaris are the big local attraction: a kick from an ostrich can reputedly kill a lion, but its bite is a bit like being savaged by a loofah.

From Oudtshoorn the route turns back to rejoin the coast at Mossel Bay. It is the largest city in the Eastern Cape, with a small port and 60 km of golden beaches. Many travellers end their Garden Route here. For others it marks merely the halfway point of the trip from Port Elizabeth to Cape Town.

Mossel Bay's early development was led by Portuguese explorers. In 1501, seeking shelter in the bay after losing his fleet in a storm, a navigator left an account of the disaster in a shoe hanging from a tree. Remarkably the report was found by the explorer to whom it was addressed, and the tree subsequently became a recognized place at which to exchange communications. The tree, now celebrated as the Post Office Tree, still stands, and beneath it a boot-shaped postbox. Elsewhere in the town the excellent Bartolomeu Diaz Museum tells the history of the place; and there are whale-watching trips in season. Beyond Mossel Bay lies the most southerly point of the African continent, Cape Agulhas. Here the Garden Route calls in at Struisbaai, a small

traditional fishing village whose harbour still buzzes with activity when the day's catch comes in. From Struisbaai the southern hemisphere's longest single beach stretches east for 14 km.

The Cape Agulhas lighthouse is South Africa's third oldest; the waters east and west of here from Cape Infanta to Danger Point have been responsible for more than 140 shipwrecks since the seventeenth century. It was off Danger Point

TOP LEFT: Struisbaai has the longest continuous white sand beach in South Africa.

TOP RIGHT: A marker stone at Cape Agulhas denotes the boundary between Indian and Atlantic oceans.

ABOVE: Take a detour in Gansbaai and get up close to a Great White Shark. Or not.

in 1852 that the sinking of HMS *Birkenhead* prompted the first use of the cry, 'Women and children first!'

There's more danger on the northern coast off the point at Gansbaai, a modest fishing port which has become world famous for its population of great white sharks. If you have the nerve, this is the place to go cage-diving in Shark Alley. Gansbaai sits at the southern end of wide Walker Bay, and at the northern extremity stands

LEFT: A colony of Jackass Penguins at Stormy Point, Betty's Bay.

BELOW: The road from Gordon's Bay to Rooi-Els.

the town of Hermanus. From June to December you can see southern right whales and other giants of the deep from the cliffs around the town. The Old Harbour Museum in Hermanus tells the story of whaling in the area. Beyond the promontory and nature reserve of Hoek-van-die-berg, Betty's Bay was the local whaling station. Now it's a marine reserve with a penguin colony on Stony Point in the town and wild dunes beyond.

Around the corner from Betty's Bay, the Atlantic Ocean rolls into the wide bowl of False Bay, enclosed by Cape Peninsula and lined on its northern shore by the suburban sprawl of Cape Town. The name False was applied by early sailors who were looking for Table Bay to the north of the Peninsula. The eastern shore of the bay is rocky and wild, with high cliffs as far as Rooi-Els. There they end in the stony outcrop of Klein-Hangklip Mountain, home to big cats

(leopards and caracal), South African black eagles and their prey – clawless otters and rock hyrax. From here on, the route sticks to the narrow foreshore at the foot of the cliffs.

From Gordon's Bay the landscape becomes more built up, and although these communities have long since been swallowed up by the expansion of Cape Town they retain their separate identities. They owe their origins to the exploitation of False Bay's natural resources – fishing, whale and seal hunting, penguin egg collection and guano mining – although most of these have been curtailed or stopped in the interests of conservation. The large colony of Cape fur seals on Seal Island in the bay attracts large schools of whales and sharks to its waters. Cape Town makes a fitting end to the route – a vibrant capital to contrast with the natural beauty of the rest of the ride. Overlooked by Table Mountain, it offers all the comforts and

excitement of city life at the end of a journey through the wonderful diversity of Africa's flora and fauna. But the Garden Route may simply have whetted your appetite for more.

BELOW LEFT: Close to Kogel Bay the Garden Route is known as Clarence Drive.

BELOW: Table Mountain and the V&A (Victoria and Alfred) Waterfront in Cape Town.

The Great Divide

Canada, USA

Length: 2,808 miles, 4,519 km
Start: Banff
Finish: Antelope Wells
Highlights: Banff, Elk River, Crossing Creek, Teton Mountains, Brooks Lake and the Pinnacle Buttes, Tie Hack Memorial, Wind River Range, South Pass City, Great Divide Basin, Park Range, Steamboat Springs, Ute Pass, Boreas Pass, Indiana Pass, Silver City

Billing itself as the Last Great American Adventure, this epic ride seeks out mountain wilderness from Alberta to New Mexico. It's an epic journey, passing through some of the most sparsely populated states in the USA.

The Great Divide is the line that separates the great oceans, the watershed, either side of which rivers run either east to the Atlantic or west to the Pacific. Characterized by the mountain chains of the Rockies and the Andes, it was only a matter of time before someone thought it would make a great MTB trail – and they were right. Three quarters of the route is on forest dirt and gravel roads with the occasional single-track. And the climbing, oh, the climbing: over the course of the full trail you will rise and fall more than 200,000 ft (60,960 metres), reaching a maximum height of 11,910 ft (3,630 metres) as you cross the Indiana Pass in Colorado.

The route starts in the mountain resort of Banff, in the heart of the Canadian Rockies, and sticks as closely as possible to the watershed. In its course it crosses the divide 30 times on its way through

British Columbia, Montana, Idaho, Wyoming and Colorado. Almost by definition the Great Divide trail avoids centres of population, and it has not been designed as a highly technical route. The priority is to lead the rider through quiet, unspoilt natural landscape. America's great rustic philosopher Henry David Thoreau might have been describing the Great Divide MTB trail when he mused, 'There are moments when all anxiety and stated toil are becalmed in the infinite leisure and repose of nature.'

The first large city after you leave Banff is Fernie in southern British Columbia. To get there the trail follows Spray River and the Spray Lakes Reservoir south of Banff, then travels further upstream with Smuts Creek and down along Smith Darrien Creek to Kananaskis Lake, then over to Elk River … this is a valley-hopping route rather than a crag-hopping one.

At Round Prairie in British Columbia the trail leaves the Elk, following the appropriately named Crossing Creek over the mountains to Bull River. This long valley is your home until Sulphur Creek takes you away, up over another pass and back down to Elk River near Fernie. You have come 160 miles of the 2,800 so far.

OPPOSITE: Downtown Banff in Alberta, Canada.

TOP RIGHT: The Great Divide trail crosses the Spray River in Alberta.

RIGHT: Calmer waters at the Elk River near Fernie.

Beyond Fernie and Eureka the Great Divide weaves its way back and forth through the Macdonald and Galton Ranges of the Rockies as if reluctant to leave Canada at all. It finally crosses the border into Montana at Roosville. Montana is the home of the Adventure Cycling Association which devised the route of the Great Divide in 1998 and publishes guides and maps for the whole trail. The trail is largely unsignposted so good maps and navigation skills are essential. Bears, wolves, mountain lions and deer are as likely to be your travelling companions as other cyclists are.

In Montana the trail passes through Whitefish and Columbia Falls on its way to the state capital Helena. Heading south-west out of Helena, it then flirts with the Montana-Idaho border, passing through Lima and Lakeview before

finally crossing the border on the watershed between Red Rock Creek and Duck Creek. The way through the Targhee National Forest leads to the Wyoming border and the Grand Teton National Park which enshrines the youngest mountain range in the Rockies, the Tetons – a mere nine million years old.

The Grand Teton Park gives way to the Teton National Forest, and the route skirts Jackson Lake before pulling east behind Rosie's Ridge and up Black Rock Creek to the foot of Angle

TOP LEFT: No prizes for guessing which state capitol we are passing in front of.

MIDDLE LEFT: The trail as it heads out of Helena, Montana.

BOTTOM LEFT: Open country along Medicine Lodge Road in Beaverhead County, Montana.

Mountain. A short haul from Togwotee Pass over to Brooks Lake gives you a trip-defining view of the Pinnacle Buttes, the tallest of them 11,496 ft (3,503 metres) high. Descending on the ridge above Brooks Lake Creek, you briefly join US Highway 26, passing the Tie Hack Memorial to the workers who cut railroad ties (sleepers) from the forests of Wyoming to feed the railroad boom of the nineteenth and early twentieth centuries.

OPPOSITE: Boundary marker at the edge of Grand Teton National Park, sited at the Hurricane Pass, Wyoming.

ABOVE: Where the buffalo once again roam, with the distinctive Teton mountain range beyond.

RIGHT: Pinnacle Buttes at the Togwotee Pass in Wyoming.

Soon the trail heads south into the Wind River Range, crossing creek after creek on its way to Pinedale, one of the most scenic sections of the trail. South of Pinedale there's insect-infested marshland, then dry desert, and in between for a few miles you are right on the Great Divide, between Little Sandy Creek and Lander Creek. They run almost parallel either side of the ridge before one turns west and the other east.

The road drops down to Highway 28, and beyond it the ghost towns of South Pass City and Atlantic City (the one that's not located in New Jersey), then strikes out across the Great Divide Basin, a desert without water or trees to shelter from the sun and dusty wind. Rawlins, 111 miles south-east of Atlantic City, marks the far end of the desert. Water is scarce elsewhere on this trail too, and you are advised to carry a water filter with you.

The Great Divide enters Colorado through the Sierra Madre Mountains. Waters from their eastern flanks eventually flow into the Gulf of Mexico through the Mississippi; those on the west become the Colorado River, which meets the sea in the Gulf of California. As the Sierra Madre becomes the Park Mountain Range the trail works down its western flank to Steamboat Springs, a winter resort so-called because its gurgling hot springs sounded like a steam boat to early trappers.

From there it follows the Yampa River upstream to Stagecoach Reservoir, then Little Morrison Creek and (big) Morrison Creek, and over Lynx Pass, another crossing of the Great Divide. It descends to cross the Colorado River at the

LEFT: A very neatly kept ghost town with the local mine on the hillside beyond, South Pass City, Fremont County, Wyoming.

TOP: On the horizon is the Wind River Range. This photo is taken from the surprisingly named Forest Road 132.

small community of Radium and climbs through mountains south of the river to Kremmling, before turning south for Breckenridge via Williams Fork Reservoir, Ute Pass, Silverthorne and Dillon Reservoir. From Breckenridge there's a painful climb over Boreas Pass (at 11,481 ft/ 3,500 metres) on Bald Mountain. It is beyond Salida and Del Norte on the Río Grande that the trail reaches its highest point, the Indiana Pass between Grayback and Bonito Mountains, where the air is thin and cold.

The place names become more Spanish in origin as the route crosses into New Mexico, a state rich in the history of both its native population and its Spanish settlers. The roads are undeniably worse here, and often impassable with mud after the heavy rains of late summer. Wintry conditions close many sections of the Great

Divide and if you plan to ride the whole trail as one journey, the window of opportunity between snow and rain is open for only two or three summer months.

Rainy season apart, it can be very dry in New Mexico, and the trail only passes through two settlements of any size. The town of Grants grew up around camps for workers on the Atlantic and Pacific Railroad. Its first wealth came from logging, and when that declined it became the celebrated Carrot Capital of the US. Its most recent economic boom followed the discovery of uranium in the area. The town, dominated by nearby Black Mesa, has an interesting mining museum.

Further south, Silver City was built on wealth from precious metal ores. The gold and silver rushes resulted in a high rate of crime, and Billy the Kid

ABOVE: Aspen Alley at Medicine Bow National Forest, Wyoming.

LEFT: Flowers growing on the verge of Road 401, south of Rawlins, Wyoming.

and Butch Cassidy's Wild Bunch all frequented Silver City's saloons. The mountains are all behind you now, and the final miles of the Great Divide Trail are on paved roads through flatlands to the Mexican border at Antelope Wells.

Truth to tell, there is nothing there besides border offices and the completist's essential photo opportunity. It is a slightly disappointing end to a magnificent ride, and many riders choose to aim instead for Columbus on the border to the east. The village was the scene of an attack by Pancho Villa which sparked the Mexican Expedition in 1916; and today it has cafés, a bank, a post office, stores and accommodation for the weary traveller.

For some it's not enough to make it from A to B; they have to *race* from A to B, and so the Tour Divide is run from north to south beginning on the second Friday every June. There is no entry fee for the Tour Divide, no registration, no prize – just glory. The clock starts, and runs continuously; there are no stages, you just start until you stop or you drop. There is no support either: competitors may shop in publicly available stores along the route but are not allowed back-up teams.

In 2016 British cyclist Mike Hall set the record for the fastest time with 13 days, 22 hours and 51 minutes, an average of 173 miles a day. Alexandera Houchin is the fastest woman ever to complete the trail with her 2019 win in 18 days, 20 hours and 26 minutes. Mere mortals in less of a hurry can expect to finish the ride in anywhere between six and ten weeks.

LEFT: Forest Road 270 near Lynx Pass in the Routt National Forest, Colorado.

BELOW: Spectacular fall colours from an aspen grove near Boreas in Colorado.

BOTTOM: Salida, Colorado, is the perfect place to stock up on provisions before heading south.

RIGHT: Marshall Pass has its place in American railroad history as it was the first crossing of the Great Divide by any railroad.

FAR RIGHT: Not the most scenic photo opportunity, but the definitive end to the Great Divide Mountain Bike cycle route – the Mexico Border Crossing.

BELOW: The dry prairie lands of New Mexico.

The Great North Trail

United Kingdom

Length: 800 miles, 1,287 km
Start: Wirksworth, Peak District
Finish: Cape Wrath or John O'Groats, Northern Scotland
Highlights: Peak District, Yorkshire Dales, Kielder Forest, Trossachs, Highlands

A new off-road route launched in 2019 takes you through the very best of British scenery. Of its 800 miles, only 16 are on busy highways. The rest follow canals, railway beds, moorland and mountain tracks, and even Roman roads.

When local authorities had still not completed the infrastructure for this route twenty years after it was first mooted, Britain's national cycling charity, Cycling UK, took matters into their own hands. In cooperation with local cycling clubs they devised their own version. It links several long-distance paths and bridleways to guide you through three National Parks and many more National Nature Reserves in some of the wildest, most beautiful landscapes of mainland Britain.

The route is divided into eight sections taking one to three days each. Although some of them run over gentler terrain or surfaced byways, overall this is regarded as a challenging mountain bike trail with tyre widths of at least 40 mm recommended. A fat-tired gravel bike is ideal for the wildest stretches. Much of the route is remote and you should not rely on telecommunications alone to find your way. Good planning is essential: the route avoids towns and cities.

The Great North Trail begins at Middleton Top, overlooking the Peak District quarry town of Wirksworth, following first an old railway bed and then the long-distance Pennine Bridleway.

This is now a rural landscape, populated by sheep and cattle, but it has been exploited for its mineral wealth for centuries. All around you are the overgrown archaeological remains of industrial processes for the extraction of ores and building stone.

There are some steep descents and ascents on this stretch, notably either side of the River Wye (not the Welsh one). Beyond Glossop, whose wealth was built on wool and cotton, the landscape is a moorland mosaic of reservoirs serving the Manchester conurbation to the west. This first leg of the North Trail ends after 80 miles with another steep drop into the Calder Valley near Hebden Bridge, once known as 'Trouser Town' because of the cloth woven there.

The next leg, 107 miles long, is a tough one. It twists in and out of lush valleys until it emerges onto weathered moorland, with views in all directions. From the wool town of Settle, the route criss-crosses the celebrated Settle–Carlisle railway with its magnificent viaducts. This section of the Great North Trail crosses the Dales of Yorkshire and East Cumbria, a series of valleys carved out of the dominant limestone geology by glaciers and rivers. Each dale, bounded by crags and waterfalls, has its own character. Above the village of Clapham, underground streams have carved spectacular cave systems now open

TOP AND MIDDLE: The trail sets off from Middleton Top in the Derbyshire Peak District and soon joins the more established Pennine Bridleway.

RIGHT: Continuing with the Pennine Bridleway, this section is near Stainforth in North Yorkshire.

OPPOSITE: The grand Ribblehead Viaduct in the Yorkshire Dales National Park.

to the public. At the head of Wensleydale (where the cheese comes from) the route enters the narrow, secret valley of Mallerstang, unspoilt and scarcely populated. Here the way gently descends past Wild Boar Fell and across the wide plain of the Upper Eden Valley, to Appleby-in-Westmorland. This small town is famed for its ancient, annual horse-trading fair and the twelfth-century castle around which it huddles in a sharp bend of the river.

North of Appleby, the trail crosses the North Pennines where, in the right weather conditions, you may see unusual clouds cascading over the ridge. These hills were mined for lead and silver by the Quaker-owned London Mining Company, and there remain shafts and ruined workshops all over the moors. The route follows the waters of the South Tyne through Alston, the highest market town in England, down to Haltwhistle. The name has nothing to do with railways but means 'high ground between two streams' – the

South Tyne and the Haltwhistle Burn by which you leave the village.

From here the route climbs again, crossing the remains of Hadrian's Wall, the northern boundary of the Roman Empire in Britain. The remote area beyond it has been described as England's Last Wilderness. It's now part of the vast Kielder Forest, the largest plantation in England and one of the largest in Europe. This stage ends deep in the forest at the head of Kielder Water, the biggest man-made lake in Britain by capacity. The section from Appleby to Kielder is 77 miles long.

Kielder is a centre for all sorts of outdoor activities including MTB trailing, and there's another trail centre on the next leg of the Great North Trail, at Glentress near Peebles. The Kielder Forest ends at the Scottish border and the trail weaves its way past the great Scottish textile towns of Selkirk, Hawick and Peebles on its way to the Scottish capital, Edinburgh. This

is a gentler but longer section, 106 miles on a mixture of lonely paths and well-used old railway beds. The final approach to Edinburgh takes you through the undulating Pentland Hills and along the Water of Leith, the river which once powered Edinburgh's flour mills. In Edinburgh you are halfway through the Great North Trail.

BELOW LEFT: Lambley Viaduct carries the South Tyne Trail across the river Tyne in Northumberland.

BELOW: Remains of the North Pennine lead-mining industry on the Durham Moors near Blanchland.

BOTTOM: Cycling through the Pentland Hills near Edinburgh.

Where the river passes under a pair of high viaducts the next stage begins. They carry a railway and a canal, both going to Glasgow, a city built on coal and steel. The canal was restored to full working order in 2000, a project which involved building an engineering marvel, the Falkirk Wheel. It's a spectacular rotating lift which raises narrow boats the 79-ft (24-metre) difference in height between two sections of the canal.

The Great North Trail follows the canal towpath all the way: a short, flat, easy day's cycling of only 52 miles. By contrast the section north of Glasgow, heading deep into the Scottish Highlands, is not for the faint-hearted: 162 miles of extreme terrain, where deep glens act as wind tunnels and exposed mountain passes can harbour snow drifts for much of the year. This, the first of three such stages, passes through the Trossachs, a large area of romantically wooded mountains and lakes beloved of Scottish author Sir Walter Scott. The bed of the old Callander–Killin branch railway takes you on a steady climb to Loch Tay. The settlements of Callander and Killin are rare oases of resources for the traveller; beyond them the way gets notably steeper and less populated. The names of natural features on the map are now in the ancient language of Scotland: Gaelic.

After Killin you ride crude tracks through the mountains and the sprawling wilderness of Rannoch Moor, more water than land, past lochs no car has ever seen. Finally, after the punishing passage of the Corrieyairack Pass, the section ends at Fort Augustus, a small village on Britain's most northerly canal, the Caledonian. Fort Augustus sits at the head of Loch Ness, the longest, deepest stretch of fresh water in Britain.

ABOVE RIGHT: The Union Canal at Viewforth, Edinburgh.

RIGHT: On every canal boater's bucket list, the spectacularly engineered Falkirk Wheel.

Cycling UK recommends that you carry an emergency radio beacon on this and the subsequent legs of the trail, especially if travelling on your own. Mobile phone reception is erratic and points of human contact few and far between. But the wild scenery through which the Great North Trail passes for the rest of its journey is without equal in Britain. Fort Augustus sits in the Great Glen geological fault which runs the entire width of Scotland, dividing the southern Highlands from the barely populated land to the north. There are no settlements at all on the next leg and only one or two near it.

It was not always thus. The mountainous far north was ruthlessly cleared of its population in the eighteenth and nineteenth centuries by landlords who could make more money from sheep and hunting. You will see the remains of abandoned homes, and this section ends after 106 miles at Oykel Bridge, where the only building is a hotel catering for the angling fraternity. Today the area is rich in wildlife and home to several species unique in Britain. There is often snow on the highest peaks here, even in August.

North of Oykel Bridge the land begins to flatten out as if finally winding down at the end of a long journey. The final section of the Great North Trail gives you a choice of destination – either the 82 miles to Cape Wrath, Britain's most north-westerly point; or the 139 to John O'Groats in the north-eastern corner of mainland Britain, from which ferries serve the Orkney archipelago to the north. Before the way splits, the route runs the length of quiet (it's in Britain's worst-selling Ordnance Survey map) Glen Cassley, a typical hunting estate whose nineteenth-century castle – built by the founder of the Royal Shakespeare Company – towers above the rough road.

Cape Wrath is only accessible by a ferry across a long inlet; and the land around it is owned by the Ministry of Defence. Bad weather or bombing practice may delay your approach to the lighthouse at the end of this arm of the trail; but the clifftop setting is spectacular and an appropriate climax to the trail. If you opt for John O'Groats, the cycling is longer but easier, mostly on surfaced minor roads. Here it's worth pedalling the extra two miles to Duncansby Head, where another lighthouse marks the true north-eastern extent of the mainland. Trains from the nearby towns of Wick and Thurso will carry you and your bicycle away from this wild end of the world and back to civilization.

OPPOSITE TOP: Latching on to the West Highland Way, the route heads down Conic Hill into the Loch Lomond and the Trossachs National Park.

OPPOSITE MIDDLE: Biking across Rannoch Moor.

OPPOSITE BOTTOM: Heading into the Rothiemurchus Forest.

ABOVE: A fine day to ascend the Glen Cassley track alongside the Cassley River in Sutherland.

RIGHT: Sea stacks at Duncansby Head, Caithness.

FAR RIGHT: The sight of the inn at John O'Groats means that you can go no further. Unless you want to take the Duncansby Head option.

Hadrian's Wall Cycleway

England

Length: 99 miles, 159 km
Start: Bowness-on-Solway, Cumbria
Finish: South Shields, Northumberland
Highlights: Lanercost Priory, Birdoswald Roman Fort, Vindolanda Roman Fort, Housesteads Roman Fort, Chesters Roman Fort

Although Roman influence extended as far north as the lowlands of Scotland, Hadrian's Wall marked the official extent of the Roman Empire in Britain. Ancient remains are all around you on a gentle bike ride along this former frontier.

Named after the Emperor Hadrian, the wall is a complex structure of walls and ditches, serviced along its length by a Roman supply road and punctuated by forts and lookout towers called milecastles. It was begun in the year AD 122 and took six years to build. Its constructors chose the narrowest part of northern England, between the Solway Firth and the Tyne estuary, a distance of only 80 miles. It's the premise for The Wall that kept out the wildlings in HBO's *Game of Thrones*.

Hadrian's Wall acted as a sort of customs check-point for merchants from lowland Scotland wishing to trade further south. It is unlikely that it could ever have withstood a concerted assault from the tribes of the north. When they repeatedly overran Hadrian's Wall during the later years of the Empire, Rome decided to quit Britain altogether. Sixteen hundred years later, a remarkable body of Roman archaeology survives.

Sustrans, the British charity which plans the country's cycling infrastructure, has designated a route along the wall's length. It can be extended to the west to include the Cumbrian coast from whose ports Romans imported and exported goods to supply its garrisons along the wall. A wooden pavilion in the village of Bowness-on-Solway marks the western end of the wall itself. Bowness was the location of the second largest fort on the wall, and the village church is built on the site of the fort's granary.

Solway Firth is a wide muddy estuary and a haven for wading birds. From Bowness the route follows its coast to Carlisle, the regional capital. The city museum has many Roman relics including a ceremonial cavalry helmet only recently discovered in a field in the area. Continuing east from the city, the more recent remains of Lanercost Priory, dating from the twelfth century, lie at the foot of a short climb to the settlement of Banks. Here you will get your first glimpse of Hadrian's Wall, still evident in the defensive ditch and roadway that lay behind it. The following long, straight section of road follows the path of the wall, and at the end of it is Birdoswald Fort, one of the many Roman garrisons along the wall's length.

A footpath from here follows the line of the wall past further remains, while the cycle route takes you north, beyond the protection of the Roman Empire. You pass near the Roman Army Museum at Walltown, and near Walltown Crags, where a dramatic stretch of the wall survives. Now the route descends gently towards Haltwhistle,

TOP: The summerhouse at the start/end of Hadrian's Wall. If you want to take a run at it you can start the cycleway further down the coast, at Siloth or even further south.

ABOVE: Vindolanda Roman Fort to the south of the Wall.

RIGHT: Campfield Marsh nature reserve on the Solway Firth.

although you may choose to remain on the minor road, the B6318 – so straight that you can be sure you are following another Roman Road. Soon after Haltwhistle the route passes Vindolanda Fort, where archaeologists have found well-preserved organic Roman remains, including footwear and hundreds of letters written on birchwood tablets. These everyday items survive because the fort was built on damp ground and the objects were buried under layers of moss, which the soldiers put down to improve their living conditions.

Not far beyond Vindolanda lies Housesteads Fort, one of the first to be excavated in modern times, from which much was learned about life as a soldier on the northern frontier. Both Housesteads and Vindolanda show evidence of a *vicus*, the civilian settlement which sprang up around military institutions supplying labour and goods. Housesteads is on a particularly well-preserved stretch of the wall itself.

Just north of the market town of Hexham is Chesters Fort, a large Roman cavalry depot which guarded a bridge over the North Tyne river. Remains of both can be seen. 'Chester', as a placename element in towns like Manchester and Colchester, is derived from the Roman word *castrum*, which means 'encampment'. The 'caster' in Lancaster and Doncaster is another variation; and it's a sign that a place was known in Roman times.

In Hexham town itself you can see Roman inscriptions on stones reused in the building of the twelfth-century Hexham Abbey, and from Hexham onwards the route follows the River Tyne to the sea; so it's downhill almost all the way. It passes through Corbridge, where remains show the town's Roman origins.

Even within the industrial conurbation of Newcastle-upon-Tyne there are stretches of Hadrian's Wall to be found, and the ride ends in spectacularly Roman style with the reconstruction of a Roman bath house at the appropriately named Wallsend. Here another large fort, Segedunum, defended the eastern end of Hadrian's border. There's a high viewing tower, and the local Metro station has signs in both English and Latin.

This is an easy ride apart from a few short sharp hills in the middle of the country. The route is almost all on well-made cycle paths or quiet minor roads, and any bicycle would be suitable for it. An athletic cyclist could easily cover it in a day, but they would miss the opportunity to immerse themselves in one of the most

important periods in Britain's history. If you want to visit some of the many archaeological sites along the way (not all of which are adjacent to the route), take a long weekend or three days. Then you can say, as Julius Caesar did about Britain in 47 BC, '*Veni, vidi, vici.*' ('I came, I saw, I conquered.')

OPPOSITE: One of the most recognizable sections of Hadrian's Wall near Housesteads, Northumberland.

ABOVE: Hadrian's Cycleway runs right along the quayside in Newcastle upon Tyne.

RIGHT: South Shields Roman fort. At Newcastle, the best of the Wall is behind you and many choose to skip the final route through urban Wallsend.

The Hebridean Way

Scotland

Length: 185 miles, 298 km
Start: Vatersay
Finish: Butt of Lewis
Highlights: Vatersay Obelisk, Kisimul Castle, Barra Airport, Eriskay ponies, South Uist mountains and machair, Our Lady of the Isles Statue, Westford Inn, Harris Distillery and Tweed, Calanais Standing Stones, Dun Carloway Broch, Butt of Lewis Lighthouse

Far out to sea, five hours by ferry from the Scottish mainland, lie the Outer Hebrides, a long chain of islands with a unique culture and few visitors. Here on the edge of the Atlantic Ocean you can escape everything except the weather.

The archipelago of the Outer Hebrides, stretched out roughly north to south, is sometimes called simply The Long Island. It is the last bastion of Scotland's native Gaelic speakers, who call their home Na h-Eileanan Siar, 'Outer Hebrides' or Na h-Eileanan an Iar, 'The Western Isles'. When the Hebrides were ruled by Norse kings they were known to mainlanders as Innse Gall, 'the Islands of Strangers'. The placenames are a unique blend of Gaelic and Norse elements.

The islands are well served by vital air and sea links. The ferry from the busy port of Oban is timed to connect with trains from Scotland's largest city, Glasgow. It sails to Castlebay, the only village on the small island of Barra. Barra was a stronghold of the MacNeil clan and there is indeed a castle, Kisimul Castle, on an island

in the bay. Barra was the location for the classic 1949 Scottish film *Whisky Galore*, and if you know the film you'll still be able to recognize some of the settings.

Neighbouring Vatersay was only recently (1991) connected to Barra by a new causeway and the route officially starts here, beside an obelisk memorializing the deaths of 350 passengers whose ship struck rocks off Vatersay and broke up in a storm in 1853. As you'll see on Vatersay, most of the roads in the Hebrides are single-lane tracks with occasional lay-bys to allow two vehicles to pass. Travelling on them becomes a matter of courtesy and mutual interest for all concerned and waves are always exchanged in passing. At the same time, with a small population and less urgency than elsewhere in the world, drivers are likely to know each other and to wind down their windows for a brief conversation. This is the pace of island life.

Returning to Barra you are faced with a choice: which way to go round the island. The road is circular, and it's the same distance by either the

TOP: From Vatersay you can take the causeway to the Isle of Barra.

MIDDLE AND OPPOSITE: The ascent to Ben Heaval on Barra, and if you have breath left when you get there, there's a breathtaking view of Castlebay.

RIGHT: Barra's airport is Tràigh Mhòr beach.

east or the west coast. Your decision may be influenced by the weather. The western shore has wonderful beaches, but the Long Island is often exposed to fierce Atlantic weather fronts. The prevailing wind is from the south-west so it is usually best to cycle the Hebridean Way from south to north; and sometimes you may be glad of the shelter which Heaval, Barra's highest hill (1,257 ft/383 metres), gives the eastern side of the island.

You leave Barra by ferry to Eriskay, a small island in the Sound of Barra famed for its ponies. But before you leave, it's worth a small detour to visit Tràigh Mhòr, 'The Big Beach' on Barra, which doubles as Barra's airstrip. A scheduled service of small planes land on the sandy beach, so the timetable is subject to change with the tides.

TOP LEFT: The causeway linking Eriskay to South Uist.

TOP: One of the fabulous Hebridean beaches at Liniclate on Benbecula.

LEFT: Chapel Road on Eriskay, whose claim to fame is one of the bumpiest football pitches in any FIFA-recognized league.

RIGHT: Most Scottish castles are formidable fortresses, but you can find a Georgian folly on Loch Scolpaig.

BELOW: The road winding through North Uist.

From Eriskay another new causeway has replaced the old ferry to South Uist. Where Barra is small and round, South Uist is long and thin, 22 miles long by as little as 3 miles wide. Its east coast is characterized by high mountains and cliffs, its west by one long beach and the unique *machair* habitat of low-growing plants.

There is only a single long, straight, relatively level road on South Uist, with short spurs leading to small communities or harbours – all are worth exploring. Now sparsely populated, the island has evidence of far greater populations in prehistoric and Viking times. At Cladh Hallan, mummified Bronze Age remains have been found, the only examples of this practice in Britain. More recently South Uist was the birthplace of Flora MacDonald, an icon of the Scottish independence movement, who helped Bonnie Prince Charlie escape after his final defeat at the Battle of Culloden in 1746.

Under the watchful eye of a statue of Our Lady of the Isles you leave South Uist for Benbecula. Halfway along the Long Island, Benbecula has a bank, shops and schools, and a large airbase, which has also brought the benefit of a public airport. Other frequent flyers here are the thousands of Canadian geese who annually use the island as a stopover on their migration route. Causeways run from Benbecula to little Grimsay, and from there across even smaller islands to North Uist, a large, low-lying island with few hills.

On a map you can see that the interior of North Uist is more water than land, a mosaic of brackish lochs and pools. The one circular road on the island sticks to the coast, and the Hebridean Way follows the longer western shore. You'll pass the Westford Inn, a rare

drinking establishment, and Balranald Nature Reserve. Throughout these unspoilt islands wildlife is abundant. The machair is a haven for corn buntings and corncrakes; and at Balranald you have a good chance of spotting a rare snowy owl or a black-billed cuckoo. Golden eagles have also been seen on North Uist.

Berneray, across a causeway from North Uist, is the departure point for the ferry to Harris, the southern half of the largest island in the Hebrides, Lewis and Harris. Harris's name derives from the Norse word for 'higher', and North

Harris has by far the steepest climbs, over barren rocky landscapes, that you'll encounter on the Hebridean Way. You'll pass the magnificent beach at Luskentyre Sands in South Harris on the way to the mountains. The island was the birthplace of Harris Tweed, at a time when every small thatched cottage had a loom in one of its rooms. The woollen cloth is currently enjoying a renaissance in the world of fashion.

RIGHT: Whisky galore at the Isle of Harris Distillery in Tarbert.

BELOW: The road to Rèinigeadal on North Harris.

By contrast, the Harris whisky distillery at Tarbert is one of the youngest in Scotland, opened in 2015. It offers tours and tastings, but beware: Harris and Lewis are staunchly Presbyterian in religious outlook and many leisure facilities, including bars, the distillery and the tees and greens of Harris Golf Club, are closed on Sundays.

Lewis, much flatter than Harris, like the Uists has a long and venerable history, exemplified by the Standing Stones of Calanais, a remarkable 5,000-year-old astronomical alignment of stones which has drawn parallels with Stonehenge. Nearby is Dun Carloway Broch, a well-preserved fortified tower built two millennia ago. The one road on Lewis runs up the beautiful west coast and finishes when it can go no further, at the Butt of Lewis, the northernmost tip. There's a clifftop lighthouse here and every chance of seeing dolphins in the waters below.

Ferries back to the Scottish mainland depart from Stornoway, the only town in the Western Isles, on Lewis's east coast. They dock in Ullapool, from where buses connect with Inverness and the rail network. Alternatively you can cycle a few miles north from Ullapool to begin the Assynt Circuit described elsewhere in this book; or you can turn around at the Butt of Lewis and cycle back to Barra. You know the way now.

BOTTOM LEFT: Standing Stones at Calanais (Callanish) on the Isle of Lewis.

RIGHT: There's a chance to see whales and dolphins from the wave-lashed cliffs at the Butt of Lewis.

BELOW: Stornoway is the largest settlement in the Hebrides, but not the only ferry port from mainland Scotland.

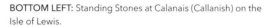

Iron Curtain Trail

Bulgaria, North Macedonia, Turkey

Length: 921 km, 572 miles
Start: Kyustendil
Finish: Tsarevo
Highlights: Kyustendil Warm Springs, Boboševo Painted Church, Prevedena and Palazlija passes, Samuil's Fortress, Popski Pass, Gotse Delchev, Zmeitsa Roman Bridge, chasm near Tešel, Široka Laka, Smolyan waterfalls, Kardzhali Town Clock, Nenkovo Cave, Ivaylovgrad Lyutitsa Fortress and Bridge, Edirne, Kayali Cliffs, Kirklareli Bazaar, Malko Tărnovo wooden houses, Kondolovo, Tsarevo Monument to the Red Army

What was once a barrier between east and west is now a long-distance cross-border trail uniting the 20 countries through which it passes. The Iron Curtain Trail is a life-affirming route and Bulgaria is its fitting conclusion.

With a total length of 7,641 km the Iron Curtain Trail is a hugely ambitious project. It is EV13, part of the EuroVelo network, and some stretches of the route exist more as proposals than completed, signposted paths. Despite that, several excellent guides to the route have already been published, and Tim Moore's funny memoir of his ride, *The Cyclist Who Went Out in the Cold*, is a must-read for anyone contemplating the adventure.

EV13 was the brainchild of Michael Cramer, a German Green Party member of the European Parliament. It starts in northernmost Norway and heads south through Finland, Russia, Estonia, Latvia, Lithuania and Poland. The middle section between former East and West Germany,

tracing the Czech-Austrian border and along the edges of Slovakia, Hungary and Slovenia, is the most complete part of the route, well signposted and on dedicated cycle paths and quiet roads.

The final 1,500 km follows the edges of Croatia, Serbia and Romania, and Bulgaria's borders with North Macedonia, Greece and Turkey. It ends on the shores of the Black Sea. The border areas through which it passes are peppered with relics of the Cold War era, and of earlier periods of international tension in history. Particularly on the communist side of the Curtain, border lands were often depopulated to make way for military defences. Consequently, they are often areas of great unspoilt beauty, undeveloped for most of the twentieth century.

Even now, 30 years after the fall of the Curtain, tourism has been slow to return to many parts of the former Eastern Bloc. For most of the route, which curls south and then east around Bulgaria, you are unlikely to see another touring cyclist; and the novelty of meeting a visitor to their country still brings out the best of Bulgarian hospitality. For tourists, Bulgarian prices are much lower than those of more developed Western European countries.

The Iron Curtain Trail runs along 1,367 km of Bulgaria's borders. A good place to pick up the trail is Kyustendil, a three-hour train journey from the capital Sofia. Like many border towns, Kyustendil has often changed hands; at different times it has been part of the Roman, Serbian

TOP: Ahmed Bey Mosque, now a museum, in Kyustendil, Bulgaria.

ABOVE: A statue of revolutionary leader Gotse Delchev in the centre of Strumica.

OPPOSITE: Looking down on Strumica, North Macedonia.

and Byzantine empires. Among its fine buildings are an eleventh-century church and a fifteenth-century mosque, and 40 warm sulphur springs in the town have made it a popular curative spa resort for centuries.

From Kyustendil the trail picks up the Struma river and follows it downstream through the pretty village of Pastuh and the quiet town of Boboševo. Boboševo is noted for its nationally important eleventh-century cloisters and fifteenth-century painted church. Near the expanding modern regional centre, Blagoevgrad, the route strikes westwards into North Macedonia. Parts of the historic region of Macedonia also lie in Bulgaria and Greece, and the first town you come to in the country is Delčevo, named after a nineteenth-century revolutionary hero revered in both Macedonia and Bulgaria.

South of Delčevo the road climbs gently towards Berovo, a small town near the source of the Bregalnica river. Notoriously polluted in its lower reaches, the river here is clean and sparkling. The town is something of a religious centre with both a monastery and a convent. Thick-socked hedonists come for the pleasures of the outdoors at nearby Berovo Lake and its surrounding mountains. Berovo also has some fame as a centre of wood carving and cheesemaking.

By contrast, Strumica in the south of North Macedonia is one of the most economically successful cities in the country, with a nightlife scene to match. The approach to Strumica is over the steep and remote Prevedena Pass (1,167 metres/3,829 ft) and its higher neighbour Palazlija Pass (1,394 metres/4,573 ft). Take care on the sharp bends of the descents.

TOP: Saint Mary of Petrich church at Asen's Fortress near Asenovgrad, Bulgaria.

LEFT: Looking down on the extensive Dospat reservoir.

From Strumica the trail follows the river of the same name as it crosses back into Bulgaria to join the Struma. Just across the border you pass Samuil's Fortress. Tsar Samuil of Bulgaria is a national hero who died of a heart attack when, after a disastrous defeat in 1014, his Byzantine enemy blinded 14,000 Bulgarian prisoners before sending them back to Samuil.

A little further on, Petrich, near the border with Greece, was the scene in 1925 of the short-lived War of the Stray Dog between the two countries. The trouble started when a Greek soldier strayed across the border in pursuit of his dog and was shot by Bulgarian guards. The war lasted five days, during which Petrich was briefly occupied by Greek troops. After Petrich you cross the Struma again and face a lengthy climb through small villages to conquer the Popski Pass (1,120 metres/3,675 ft), a quiet road of variable surface which crosses cliffs and can get snow as early as October. There are hotels and restaurants at the summit, and a bronze sculpture of soldiers.

The descent, with grand views, takes you to the Mesta Valley and the town of Gotse Delchev, named like Delčevo in Macedonia after the

ABOVE: A minaret in the middle of town reveals that Dospat has a large muslim community.

ABOVE RIGHT: The Teshel Reservoir in the Smolyan region.

RIGHT: A reconstructed Roman bridge in the village of Široka Laka, Bulgaria.

revolutionary hero Gotse Delchev. Delchev fought to liberate Bulgaria from Ottoman rule and was shot by Turkish police in 1903. His namesake town has unpromising outskirts but a charming old centre. Climbing out of the town you reach the twin mosques of Dolno Dryanovo – this is a historic area of Muslim population in Bulgaria. There's an early holy site just outside the town, where prehistoric carved stone heads have been discovered. Further on, Dospat and its minaret sit on a hillside at one end of the second largest man-made reservoir in Bulgaria, Dospat Lake. The lake sits on top of a German military airfield left behind after World War II.

From Dospat the trail enters one of its most beautiful sections, hopping from valley to valley through gorges and between cliffs. Look out for the Roman bridge at Zmeitsa, the chasm near Tešel, and the traditional village of Široka Laka with its thick, whitewashed walls and a reputation for fine folk music. A hard climb from here and

a harder descent take you to Smolyan, the highest city in Bulgaria. It's a modern industrial conurbation, but surrounded by mountains and some wonderful waterfalls, including the Waterfalls Canyon just to the west.

The trail crosses the wide Arda valley to Madan, a lead-mining town for two and a half millennia, and climbs a snaking road over the pass to Tsatsarovtsi. Beware of the unguarded edges and sharp turns of the descent. At the bottom lies Zlatograd, Bulgaria's most southerly city and not its most beautiful. However, it does contain the Ethnographic Area Complex, a centre of traditional costume, music and crafts. From here the route sticks to the hills north and west of the Vărbica river as it descends towards Kardzhali.

This part of Bulgaria was historically part of Turkey and 62% of the population still consider themselves Turkish. The discovery of zinc and lead ores in the area have boosted the city's

ABOVE LEFT: The meandering Arda river in the Rhodope mountains, Bulgaria.

ABOVE: The village of Zlatograd is only 3 km from the Bulgaria-Greece border.

OPPOSITE TOP: Kardzhali in Bulgaria has an impressive history museum.

economy; but so too has tourism. The centre is lively and attractive, and the town clock plays the Bulgarian Revolutionary Hymn every hour. There is a good museum of the town's history, and 15 km north of the city lies the ancient Thracian city of Perperikon, built into the cliffs. A prehistoric man-made cave near the town has been compared to Stonehenge for its astronomical alignment: on one day of the year a ray of sunlight shines through an opening to illuminate the back wall.

East of Kardzhali the trail cuts overland to Ivaylovgrad, with some steep ascents in beautiful countryside, through Krumovgrad and pretty villages like Pelin and Perunika. There is Thracian, Roman and Byzantine archaeology here. The walls of the twelfth-century Lyutitsa Fortress, approached via a sixteenth-century stone bridge, still stand 6 metres (20 ft) high and 1.75 metres (6 ft) thick, and are built on earlier, ninth-century remains.

From Ivaylovgrad the route turns unexpectedly northwards across the Arda river to reach Svilengrad, where there are no fewer than four castles. This is a busy border town at the triangular meeting point of Bulgaria, Turkey and Greece, and the Iron Curtain Trail turns away just

ABOVE: Perperikon is the site where Medokos declared himself King of Thrace in 424 BC.

RIGHT: Utroba Cave near Kardzhali is also known as 'the womb cave'.

before the town to cross over into Greece. You are not allowed to carry milk, cheese or sausages over the border. You rejoin the Arda river in the country; and after only 60 km you go through customs again, this time into Turkey.

Edirne, the first Turkish town you come to, takes its name from the Roman emperor Hadrian and some of the Roman city walls still survive. The town is famous for its many old mosques, minarets and caravanserais (the Asian name for a roadside inn, typically found on the Silk Road), as well as Ottoman remains including Edirne Palace.

The route through Turkey is a welcome low-lying one, but on remote and sometimes poorly surfaced and signposted roads. It connects Edirne with Lalapaşa and its twin minarets, Kayali with its cliff formations, and Kirklareli with its fourteenth-century bathhouse and bazaar. Then, one last time, you cross the border back into Bulgaria and continue to Malko Tărnovo, a small Bulgarian town with many charming traditional wooden houses. From Tărnovo the road goes through some

tight hairpin bends as it descends to the meandering Veleka river. There's a 10% incline through woodland after you cross it and before you emerge in the village of Gramatikovo and, a little further on, Kondolovo, a village where time seems to have stood still since the late nineteenth century. As you descend gently from here you get your first views of the Black Sea, and before you know it you are in Tsarevo, journey's end. The water in the bay here warms up faster than anywhere else on the Bulgarian coast, and Bulgarians love to visit its pretty harbour. Note that the nearest railway station is in Burgas, 65 km to the north.

The Iron Curtain Trail is a fascinating opportunity to compare several cultures relatively unknown to Western Europeans in a landscape of magnificent mountains and unfamiliar architectural styles. If you're planning to tackle it, make sure you have up-to-date information about the route, which is liable to change until it is finally agreed by all parties. Bulgaria still operates internal checkpoints on some roads.

Be sensitive to local political and religious history, but enjoy the opportunity to sample new dishes, old customs and warm hospitality.

TOP: Ivaylovgrad dam on the Arda river in Bulgaria.

ABOVE: Historic bridge in Edirne, Turkey. Edirne was founded by the Roman emperor Hadrian, whose work appears elsewhere in this book.

FAR LEFT: The courtyard of the Bayezid II Mosque (1488) in Edirne. Today it is a museum dedicated to the history of medicine.

LEFT: The main sreet in Kirklareli, Turkey.

BELOW: Looking out on the Black Sea resort of Tsarevo in Bulgaria.

Isle of Wight, Round-the-Island Cycle Route

United Kingdom

Length: 58 miles, 93 km
Start/Finish: Cowes
Highlights: Osborne House, Isle of Wight Steam Railway, Bembridge Fort, the Needles, Shalfleet

England's largest island became a popular holiday destination after Queen Victoria built herself a summer retreat here in 1845. A circuit of the island makes a good day trip, or part of a longer holiday.

Before Queen Victoria, the island was very rural in character, with a fascinating history stretching back to Neolithic times. It was known as *Vectis* by the great Roman historian Ptolemy, and several Roman villas have been excavated. Often bearing the brunt of attacks from invading forces, the island also has the remains of defensive systems from many periods of its history when it had to withstand raids by Vikings, Spanish, French and German forces.

The circular route round the island steers as far as possible clear of main roads in favour of quieter byways. You can travel either clockwise or anticlockwise and start from anywhere on the route. Of the three main ferry terminals on the island, Yarmouth and Cowes are on the route, and Ryde only a mile north of it.

Heading east from Cowes the clockwise route takes you close to Queen Victoria's summer home, Osborne House, where she died in 1901. South of Ryde you will cross the island's 15-mile-long railway network at Smallbrook Junction. There are two lines: one, from Ryde to Shanklin, operates as part of the national network but uses former London Underground trains because of the line's narrow tunnels. The other, running

between Smallbrook Junction and Newport, is a heritage steam railway.

The route rarely rises more than 300 ft (91 metres) above sea level as it follows the coast, reaching a maximum of around 500 ft (152 metres) as it curls inland between Bembridge in the east and the cliffs of Blackgang in the south. Bembridge Fort is a relic of the time in the nineteenth century when England feared an attack by Napoleon III of France. After Blackgang, the road descends gently to Afton, passing through some outstanding scenery. From Afton it's worth a three-mile detour to see the famous chalk stacks of the Needles at the western end of the 'lettuce leaf'.

The island is almost bisected by the river Yar, which you cross at Yarmouth. From Yarmouth back to Cowes the route passes through a succession of pretty villages, including quiet Shalfleet. Here, in 2009, a large hoard of gold and silver Iron Age treasure was found, proving the presence of a Celtic tribe on the Isle of Wight. A short spur from the main route leads to Shalfleet Quay, a small harbour on an inlet of the sea where, perhaps, the hoard was originally offloaded.

For those pressed for time there is a shorter circular route which omits the eastern and western extremities of the island. There are also eight traffic-free cycle paths on the island which do not form part of the Round-the-Island route.

TOP: Osborne House, one of Queen Victoria's residences.

MIDDLE: Bembridge has a modern RNLI lifeboat station.

BOTTOM: Cowes, famous for the Cowes Week regatta.

OPPOSITE: Freshwater Bay and Tennyson Down. The great poet lived at Farringford House for almost 40 years.

The Katy Trail

Missouri, USA

Length: 237 miles, 381 km
Start: Machens
Finish: Clinton
Highlights: St Charles station and town centre, Femme Osage Creek bridge, Missouri Meerschaum Company, Hermann, the Grand Bluffs, Jefferson City Capitol, Boonville's Katy Bridge, Boone's Lick, Sedalia Station

The Katy Trail is the jewel in the crown of America's rail-to-trail programme. Running alongside the mighty Missouri for most of the trail's 237 miles, it passes through historic riverside settlements and wild natural habitats.

This is the longest rail trail in the US. It follows the trackbed of part of the old Missouri, Kansas and Texas Railroad – the MKT, the KT, or Katy for short. Originally formed in 1865, it was the first railroad company to enter Texas from the north, and today its surviving routes form part of the Union Pacific Railroad.

The stretch over which the Katy Trail runs was abandoned after the latest in a series of catastrophic Missouri floods, causing damage not considered worth repairing by the railroad company in 1986. Work began soon afterwards on converting it into a leisure trail, but its opening was delayed by further water damage in the Great Flood of 1993, when both the Mississippi and the Missouri rivers burst their banks. In its present form the Katy Trail was opened in three stages between 1996 and 2011.

The surface is good throughout its length, a compacted limestone which only becomes difficult in the sort of torrential downpour you wouldn't want to be cycling in anyway. As a former railbed it is delightfully flat. There are 26 trailstops along the route, ranging from simple shelters to former stations with toilet facilities and information about local attractions. Most of the towns along this stretch of the Missouri are on the south bank. The Katy Trail sticks to the north side, passing largely through rural countryside and natural landscapes.

The trail begins in Machens, a small farming community on a narrow strip of land between the Missouri and Mississippi, about 15 miles from their confluence north of St Louis. The first stop is one of the largest trailstops on the route, the beautiful old station building at St Charles. St Charles, founded in 1769, has a handsome centre of old buildings. An early trail, the Boone's Lick Road, started here and ended in Franklin, where the Santa Fe Trail took over; St Charles was consequently the gateway for the exploration of the Wild West. The town was Lewis and Clark's last taste of civilization before they headed west in 1804. The Katy Trail now follows the Boone's Lick path along the northern bank of the Missouri, and it follows part of the Lewis and Clark National Historic Trail too.

The trail has to cross many tributaries of the Missouri, including Femme Osage Creek at Defiance, where one of many former rail

BELOW: A former Katy depot in St Charles, Missouri.

BOTTOM: The Missouri river bridge at Hermann, Missouri.

bridges makes the crossing. The Katy Trail is in the US Railbank: it must remain possible to reconnect it to the national rail network should the need arise. So it's not only a pleasure but a requirement that such bridges remain in place.

Further upstream, the city of Washington was a steamboat hub for transportation up and down the river. It has more buildings on the Register of Historic Places than anywhere else in Missouri. And thanks to the continuing presence of the Missouri Meerschaum Company it can still stake the enviable claim to being 'The Corncob Pipe Capital of the World'.

Hermann on the other hand, further west, is the self-styled 'Sausage Capital of Missouri'. As the name suggests, it was founded by German settlers hoping to establish a Teutonic colony in the heart of America. They brought with them their knowledge of both wurst and wine; the town's vineyards account for a third of the state's wine production. For good measure Hermann also celebrates its German-style breweries with a month-long Oktoberfest.

RIGHT: Limestone cliffs above the trail at Rocheport, Missouri.

BOTTOM: The initials on the trail marker, MKT, stand for Missouri, Kansas and Texas.

Beyond Hermann the trail passes below Missouri's Grand Bluffs, cliffs eroded by the river in an earlier age.

Further along the route you come to Jefferson City, Missouri's state capital and the second city on the trail to be named for a president, after its residents rejected the name Missouriopolis. The imposing Capitol building was dedicated in 1924, but Lewis and Clark are known to have passed by the bluff on which it stands 120 years earlier. Jefferson sits roughly halfway along the Katy Trail.

Before the Katy Trail was laid out, Columbia, the largest city in the state, converted a disused spur of the line for bicycle use. Confusingly it was called the MKT Trail, and where it intersects with the Katy Trail north-west of Jefferson City you can follow it through beautiful countryside right into downtown Columbia.

Further upstream, trains had to cross the river to get to Boonville on an impressive truss bridge with a lifting central section which allowed river traffic to pass. Known as the Katy Bridge, it is under restoration at the time of writing. Cyclists currently use the adjacent Boonslick Bridge, from which there is a better view of the Katy Bridge than if you were on it. The original Boone's Lick, a salt spring to which Boone's Lick Road originally

led, is a little further upstream near Arrow Rock. It was named after the sons of famous frontiersman Daniel Boone who first marked out the road. But at Boonville the Katy Trail turns away from the Missouri River and heads for Sedalia. The Sedalia trailhead is a grand former station and welcome centre for the town which hosts the annual Missouri State Fair.

ABOVE: The converted Katy depot in Sedalia.

ABOVE LEFT: The Columbia (MO) spur of the MKT spans 9 miles and connects to the Katy Trail at McBaine, Missouri.

TOP: There's a historic rail bridge over the Missouri at Boonville, with a lifting midsection.

Throughout its existence, Sedalia has been a town that people have passed through – cattlemen, railroad workers, travelling salesmen – and in the nineteenth century it had something of a reputation for vice. There were so many brothels that the town's services were paid for out of the fines levied on red light activities. The ladies worked in bars, the bars hired musicians, and it was in Sedalia that piano player Scott Joplin honed his craft. The town hosts an annual Scott Joplin Ragtime Festival.

Thirty-five miles further down the line, Clinton is named not after a third president but a former New York governor, DeWitt Clinton. He promoted the Erie Canal, which opened up access to the eastern seaboard for midwestern farmers and their goods via the MKT Railroad and other lines: a great many towns are named either DeWitt or Clinton in his honour. Here the Katy Trail ends – for now. There are detached rail-to-trail parts of the old MKT in Dallas and Houston TX, and in Tulsa OK. Perhaps one day the whole route will be reunited.

ABOVE: A former MKT tunnel at Rocheport, Missouri.

RIGHT: Hotel Bothwell has a vintage neon sign to attract visitors in downtown Sedalia.

Ring of Kerry

Ireland

Length: 171 km, 105 miles
Start/Finish: Killarney town centre
Highlights: Killorglin, Kerry Bog Village Museum, Ballycarbery Castle, Valentia Island dinosaur footprints, Atlantic Telegraph memorial, Coomakista Pass, Staigue Fort, Moll's Gap, Muckross House and Gardens

This perennially popular loop around Ireland's Iveragh Peninsula can be busy in high season, but offers a variety of landscapes including rolling fields, coastal roads and a mountain or two; and glimpses of Irish history, including the prehistoric and the pre-human.

The Iveragh Peninsula is the largest of the fingers of land which jut out into the Atlantic Ocean in County Kerry, Ireland's south-western corner. It can bear the brunt of Atlantic storms but also benefits from the warm air of the Gulf Stream. It is good green farming country, huddled around the MacGillycuddy's Reeks mountain range, which stands in the centre of it.

FAR LEFT: A statue of King Puck, by the bridge at Killorglin.

BELOW: The Caragh River as viewed from the Ring of Kerry.

OPPOSITE: Ireland has many romantic ruins, including Ballycarbery Castle at Cahersiveen.

The Ring of Kerry is a permanent feature of many coach tours of Ireland, and by common consent they all drive it in an anticlockwise direction – much of the road is too narrow for two coaches to pass by each other. The cycle trail shares these public roads, but there's always room for a bicycle in either direction. There is plenty of accommodation along the route and it's worth spending two or three days to complete it.

The route is well signposted – look for a distinctive crown-shaped logo. It departs from Killarney on the N72, following the River Laune as it leaves Lough Leane and makes its short journey to the sea beyond Killorglin. This is a busy stretch of road and, if you prefer, there is a quieter, prettier route to Killorglin via the village of Beaufort on the other side of the river. Near Beaufort are the Dunloe Ogham stones, a set of medieval grave markers with inscriptions carved in the Ogham alphabet.

In Killorglin, look for the statue to King Puck – a crowned goat – before you turn left onto the N70. In an ancient celebration, held anually, a wild goat (known as a 'puck') is crowned king of the town for three days before being returned to the Irish hills. Just beyond the Kerry Bog Village Museum you cross the River Caragh where it meets the sea in Dingle Bay. Past the village of Glenbeigh you get your first stiff climb, and your first glimpse of the open sea, the North Atlantic Ocean. By the roadside is a memorial to the hero of an earlier Irish uprising, John Golden.

OPPOSITE: Panoramic views over Abbey, Deenish and Scariff islands from Coomakista Pass on the Iveragh peninsula.

TOP: The Garden of the Pyramids of Sneem on the Sneem River.

RIGHT: The Horeshoe in Kenmare. It may slow your progress, but stopping at pubs is a cultural necessity.

The official Ring of Kerry follows the N70 throughout its length, but at Cahersiveen, birthplace of national political hero Daniel O'Connell, it's worth making a short uphill detour to Cahergall, an impressive seventh-century stone fortress, or *cashel*. On the way back you'll see Ballycarbery Castle, the sixteenth-century stronghold of the McCarthy clan.

Just beyond Cahersiveen a longer detour (about 26 km/16 miles) will take you by ferry to charming Valentia Island. It's a hospitable place now, although this may not always have been the case – on the north coast of Valentia you can see the fossilized remains of dinosaur footprints in rocks on the shore. Before you leave the island by a bridge at the southern end, look for the

memorial to the eastern terminal of the first ever transatlantic telegraph cable. There are dramatic ocean views from here.

Back on the N70 you descend to Ballinskelligs Bay and Waterville, a Victorian holiday resort still popular today. Charlie Chaplin took an annual holiday here for over ten years from the 1950s to the 1970s. After Waterville the Ring of Kerry climbs Coomakista Pass, where your reward is the freewheeling descent to Caherdaniel and terrific views of the rocks and islands offshore. Here there's another, less well preserved stone fortress. These impressive circular structures are reminders of a lawless time when even farms had to be fortified.

Now you're well over halfway around the Ring of Kerry, following the southern coast of the peninsula. Take a break at O'Carroll's Cove, a stunning secret beach of sand and blue water with a singular café. At Castlecove a short spur will lead you to the peninsula's best-known fort, Staigue, halfway up a hillside with commanding views to the south.

The Ring heads slightly inland before dropping down into the town of Sneem. The name means 'knot' in Gaelic and probably refers to the twisting currents in the sea here where the Sneem river meets the tides of Kenmare Bay. Given Ireland's troubled political relationship with Britain in the past, it is something of an irony that the first chief of the British Secret Service Bureau, William Melville, was born here in 1850.

From Sneem the Ring hugs the coast to Kenmare, curling around the tranquil wooded natural harbour of Leckeen, the mouth of the Blackwater river. Look out for the Pequeña Fortaleza, a folly in the form of a small ruined castle. Kenmare is a bustling, pretty town with a prehistoric stone circle a short walk from its centre. Its Irish name, *An Neidín*, means 'the little nest' and it's a good idea to stop and take refreshments here ahead of the greatest cycling challenge of the Ring of Kerry: Moll's Gap.

As you leave Kenmare on the N71 the road climbs relentlessly towards the summit of Moll's Gap, a dramatic pass through the MacGillycuddy's Reeks (Ireland's highest mountain range, of which Carrauntoohil is highest at 1,039 metres/3,407 ft, and with ten peaks over 914 metres/3,000 ft). There's a café at the top, and the descent, in two stages, is just as challenging, as the road snakes down to Lough Looscaunagh. Beyond the lough, Ladies View offers a panorama of the lakes of Killarney National Park laid out below you.

Now the road tumbles down to the park, meeting it alongside the Upper Lake. At Muckross Lake you'll pass romantic Torc Waterfall, where the waters drain from Torc Mountain. The gardens of Muckross House, a Victorian mansion, are worth a visit, particularly at rhododendron time. After the ruined fifteenth-century Muckross Abbey you return to civilization and the outskirts of Killarney, where the circle of the Ring of Kerry is completed.

ABOVE: The majestic MacGillycuddy's Reeks, the highest mountains in Ireland.

TOP RIGHT: Looscaunagh Lough in the Killarney National Park, viewed from the head of the lake.

RIGHT: Muckross House located on the Muckross peninsula between Muckross Lake and Lough Leane in Killarney.

La Farola

Cuba

Length: 52 km, 32 miles
Start: Cajobabo
Finish: Baracoa
Highlights: Cajobabo, Las Guásimas, Mirador de Alto de Cotilla, Yumurí, El Yunque de Baracoa

One of the great engineering achievements of the Communist Revolution in Cuba, La Farola carves an extraordinary, twisted route through and over the mountainous east of the island. It's an exhilarating (which means exhausting) challenge for the cyclist.

When Fidel Castro ordered the construction of La Farola he made good on a project begun but abandoned by his predecessor, the dictator Fulgencio Batista. Until it was completed in 1965, Cuba's oldest settlement Baracoa was cut off from the rest of the country, walled in by the impenetrable heights of the Cuchillas de Baracoa, 'the Blades of Baracoa', and accessible only from the sea. Baracoa's isolation made it a haven for many, and today its multicultural population includes Jamaicans, Haitians and the only surviving descendants of Cuba's indigenous Taíno people.

Strictly speaking La Farola refers to the 160-km highway from Guantánamo to Baracoa. But it is the 52-km section beyond Cajobabo, where the road turns inland and climbs the Sierra del Purial, which really excites cyclists.

The road begins by following the deep valley of the Río Jojo, climbing past a viewpoint at Veguita del Sur and the scattered settlement of Las Guásimas in a broad bend of the river. From there it leaves the Jojo and starts to climb steeply, clinging to cliffsides and winding round mountain spurs to the 550-metre (1,804-ft) summit at Alto de Cotilla – where there is the most welcoming sight in the world, a cafeteria. Here too is the view that rewards the climb.

From Alto de Cotilla there's a thrilling freewheel down to the village of Yumurí and the Yumurí Valley, which the road crosses on one of eleven bridges that the construction of the road demanded. A lesser climb out of the valley takes La Farola via a tortuous route to the valley of the Río Miel. From this point onwards it's downhill all the way, through a succession of villages, to the mouth of the Miel at Baracoa.

Baracoa is a delight, a maze of lively streets that beg to be wandered through. It has not one but three forts, built to defend the isolated town from marauding pirates. If you have any energy left you can walk up El Yunque, the anvil-shaped mountain which towers above; and there are shorter walks to waterfalls. But you may prefer to sit quietly and reflect on the wild and beautiful landscape through which you have just travelled.

LEFT: A view over Baracoa looking towards the table-top mountain El Yunque.

OPPOSITE: La Farola winds through the mountains from Cajobabo to Baracoa.

The Lakeland Loop

England

Length: 40 miles, 64 km
Start/Finish: Broughton-in-Furness
Highlights: Broughton-in-Furness, Coniston Water, Little Langdale Tarn, Wrynose Pass, Dunnerdale, The Old Man of Coniston

England's three highest mountains sit in the Lake District. The region has a magnetic attraction for road cyclists ready for a challenge. With gradients of up to 25%, the Lakeland Loop will have you reaching for the granny gears.

While weekend cyclists may prefer a nice flat ride along a river, there are hardened cyclists who like nothing better than the sweat and toil of a punishing climb. For those inclined, this is the ideal loop, with three stiff climbs over 40 miles as it circumnavigates a hillwalkers' favourite, the Old Man of Coniston.

Broughton-in-Furness, with a population of less than 600, is one of the ten smallest towns in England. It has held market town status since at least the eleventh century when it was recorded in the Domesday Book. Today it still sustains two pubs, the Old King's Head and the Black Cock Inn, and makes a good place to start and finish this bracing round. It is the nearest point to the rail network too – Foxfield station, two miles to the south, is a request stop on the Cumbrian coastal line, so make sure someone knows you want to get off here.

OPPOSITE: Fell Foot Farm, Little Langdale, near Ambleside.

RIGHT: The Black Cock Inn at Broughton.

FAR RIGHT: Wrynose Pass looking towards Hardknott Pass.

ABOVE RIGHT: Coniston Water from Furness Fells.

From Broughton the trail leaves on Keppleway Hill and makes its way over a pass between Blawith Knott and Great Burney, gaining 400 ft (122 metres) in a mile. It drops down again to cross the River Crake beside the Red Lion Inn at Lowick Bridge, and follows the river to its source at the foot of Coniston Water.

Coniston Water, five miles long, was the scene for several water speed records achieved by Sir Malcolm Campbell and his son Donald between 1939 and 1959. In quieter times Arthur Ransome set his *Swallows and Amazons* children's novels here. The artist and philosopher John Ruskin made his home in Brantwood House on the east shore, which the cycle route now follows.

A 2.5-mile incline takes you up another 450 ft (137 metres) over Hawkshead Hill. From here the road drops down to the River Brathay and follows it upstream through the valley of Little Langdale. Now the trouble starts: at the well-named Fell Foot Farm, the route starts to climb to Wrynose Pass, a 920-ft (280-metre) ascent in only 1.75 miles, with a maximum gradient of 25%. The descent, on a more gentle gradient, is fun

and well deserved after Wrynose, following the River Duddon through Dunnerdale Forest. At Duddon Bridge, a short stretch on a busy main road takes you back to Broughton. Did we mention the two pubs?

The Loire Valley

France

Length: 385 km, 239 miles
Start: Saint-Brévin-les-Pins
Finish: Orléans
Highlights: Les Machines de L'Île (Nantes), Châteaux d'Ancenis and de Serrant, Saumur, Tours, Châteaux d'Amboise, de Chenonceau, de Chambord and de Meung-sur-Loire, Labyrinthe de Beaugency, Orléans

The stately Loire flows past some of the finest palaces in Europe and through some of France's grandest cities. Historically navigable from the Atlantic Ocean to Orléans, a cycle along its banks makes a comfortable week-long holiday.

At 1,012 km the Loire is France's longest river, rising in the French Alps in the south-east of the country and flowing northwards to Orléans, where it turns west and heads for the ocean. Shallow-bottomed boats were able to sail up the Loire from the sea to the quayside in Orléans without the need for canals or locks, so cyclists making the same journey can be sure of a flat ride all the way – the route rises barely 100 metres (328 ft) over its 385-km length.

Historically the Loire was seen as the dividing line between the north and south of France; a useful border for quarrelling factions on either side of it. Castles were built along its banks, which over time became aggrandized to the magnificent Loire châteaux which survive today. There are over a thousand of them, a rough average of one stately pile for every kilometre of river.

This is a very popular trail and several sections of the Loire are offered by travel firms as cycling package holidays. The mouth of the Loire is the start of one of Europe's long-distance EuroVelo bike trails, EV6. After the Loire it continues via a stretch of the Rhône to the Danube, which it follows all the way to its end on the Black Sea. The whole route, like the Loire Valley, is relatively level and easy to ride, and the journey from western to eastern Europe is a slide show of changing cultures and histories.

Reasonably fit cyclists can easily complete the stretch from the estuary to Orléans in six days at an average of less than 65 km a day. Families with younger children might prefer to do shorter stages: you can skip parts of it by taking the Interloire train service, which runs between Nantes and Orléans and adds an extra carriage just for bicycles during the summer. The same service will take you back to your starting point when you finish the trip.

Although many people begin or end the route in Nantes, the official terminus is Saint-Brevin-les-Pins, a smart town on a promontory between the river and the sea. Saint-Brevin developed as a holiday resort for workers from Nantes and their rich employers. It has sumptuous villas, a casino, and a coastline of sand dunes – the pine trees, 'les pins' in its name, were originally planted to stabilize serious coastal erosion which swallowed up parts of the town.

OPPOSITE: The medieval castle of Oudon sits on high ground overlooking the Loire.

BELOW: Saint-Brevin-les-Pins at the mouth of the Loire.

BOTTOM: Loire houseboats in Nantes.

Before ships became too large for river navigation, Nantes was the busiest port in France, thanks to the traffic of goods up and down the Loire. The city grew up around a large island in the river, which is still its creative heart. It is the site, among other things, of the remarkable Les Machines de L'Île, a steampunk wonderland of mechanical marvels including a full-size robotic elephant which you can ride on. If nothing else, it will put the engineering complexities of your bicycle in perspective. Upstream from Nantes you'll see the castles of Oudon and Ancenis, examples of the original defensive functions of many Loire châteaux. Ancenis's massive round-towered gateway earned it the nickname 'the key to Brittany', for which it was once the entry point.

LEFT: Château de Serrant started off as a medieval fortress but received a Renaissance rebuild.

BELOW: Angers sits on the banks of the river Maine in the department of Maine-et-Loire.

Just outside Angers, the Château de Serrant shows how many such castles developed when they were no longer required for defensive purposes. It stands on the foundations of the old fortress and sits within its moat, but was completely remodelled in the seventeenth century. Now the private home of a Belgian prince, it is open to the public, who can admire its huge library and a bedroom decorated for Napoleon (although he only visited the castle for two hours). Angers sits at the strategically important confluence of the Maine and Loire rivers and has its own castle, the thirteenth-century stronghold of the royal Plantagenet family. From here on, and for the rest of the trail, you are in the Val de Loire UNESCO World Heritage Park.

Saumur boasts a tenth-century castle and France's largest prehistoric burial chamber. During World War II Saumur was defended by cadets of the local cavalry school, who are remembered in the name of one of the town's bridges; there's also a Cavalry Museum in the town. Tunnels created when the building stone for the town was excavated are now used as cellars by the local wine producers. The Manoir de Launay on the edge of Saumur is typical of the sort of grand French farmhouse which, though not entitled to be a château, wishes it

were. René, Duke of Anjou, bought it in 1444 and staged jousting tournaments here. Upstream from Saumur, Azay-le-Rideau is a fairy-tale castle on an island in the Loire tributary the Indre.

Tours, the largest city on the Loire, has been an important river crossing for thousands of years. It sits in an excellent defensive position, on a long, thin spit of land between the Loire and its tributary the Cher. Tours was a large Roman metropolis, and the remains of the Roman amphitheatre stand next to Tours' magnificent Gothic cathedral. The city stands on a pilgrim route to Santiago de Compostela in Spain, and Tours has its own famous saint, St Martin. The city's Woodrow Wilson Bridge commemorates the presence here during World War I of a large

ABOVE LEFT: Château d'Azay-le-Rideau.

ABOVE: On the hill is the Château de Saumur; in the foreground the Cessart Bridge over the Loire.

RIGHT: Soaring over the city of Tours is the Cathédrale Saint-Gatien.

contingent of US soldiers and airmen, several of whom married local women. In October the city is the finishing line for an annual bike race from Paris – the Paris–Tours one-day classic – one of the oldest cycling races in the world, which started up in 1896.

The lands of the Loire between Tours and Orléans are occupied by some of the most impressive of the Loire châteaux. Mary Queen of Scots spent her early life here in the Château Royal d'Amboise, and Leonardo da Vinci spent his final years in the Château de Clos Lucé nearby. If you only make one detour during your trip, make it to Chenonceau, one of the Loire's most beautiful châteaux, which spans the river Cher near Amboise.

The Château de Chaumont with its annual Garden Festival, the gleaming Château de Chambord and its park, and the austere Château de Meung-sur-Loire all combine to give a sense of the competition among their owners to impress with wealth and status.

It's not all castles, though – the Royal Château de Blois must compete with the nearby Roman Land theme park; and near Beaugency there's a large maze with a fairy-tale theme by day and occasional haunted late-night events. What scary

TOP LEFT: The one-day classic bike race Paris-Tours crosses the bridge at Amboise.

ABOVE: Two views of the UNESCO World Heritage Site Château Chenonceau.

ABOVE: The Château de Chambord is the largest in the Loire valley.

monster lurks around the next corner? Well, some towers of a very different kind: the cooling towers of the Saint-Laurent Nuclear Power Plant.

This trail ends in Orléans, the region's administrative centre. Joan of Arc, the Maid of Orléans, helped to lift the city's siege by the English in 1429. All was forgiven by the time the city renamed one of its bridges after British King George V, in recognition of Britain's help during World War I. Joan of Arc is still revered here, and you can visit her house, which, like many Orléans treasures, was destroyed during World War II. The Germans had made Orléans a central rail hub and it was heavily bombed by the American Airforce in 1944 as part of the Allies' drive to liberate France. It was reconstructed

soon afterwards. The Forêt d'Orléans is France's largest National Forest.

This is an easy, well-signposted trail suitable for the whole family. Even detours to châteaux inland from the banks of the Loire are gentle of gradient and short in distance. The route intersects with several other long-distance cycle routes through France, including EV1, The Atlantic Coast of Europe, and EV3, The Pilgrims Route from Trondheim in Norway to Santiago in Spain. You won't want to stop.

ABOVE: In the foreground is the Royal Château de Blois.

RIGHT: Orléans' Sainte-Croix cathedral viewed down the rue Jeanne d'Arc.

London to Paris avoiding the traffic

England, France

Length: 200 miles, 320 km
Start: London
Finish: Paris
Highlights: Greenwich, Outwood Windmill, Bluebell Railway, Lewes, Newhaven Fort, Neufchâtel-en-Bray, Forges-les-Eaux, Gournay-en-Bray, Vexin Français, Bois de Boulogne, Eiffel Tower

Once you've followed a few established trails, many cyclists are tempted to start devising their own. The route between the capital cities of London and Paris is a popular challenge. Can you do better than the official route, the Avenue Verte?

One of the great advantages of cycling as a mode of transport is its flexibility – its ability to go where cars and trains cannot, and to adapt quickly when a new path presents itself or an old one is blocked off. Part of the pleasure of cycling lies in the creation of new journeys; but particularly on long-distance routes, competing factors influence a cyclist's decisions. Which is the shortest? Which is the flattest? Which is the prettiest? And perhaps most important of all, which is the quietest?

The London–Paris route attracts a lot of attention. Apart from individuals making the trip, there are several mass rides each year to raise money for charities. The journey is complicated by the need to cross the English Channel somehow, somewhere. Of the many competing routes from London to Paris, one combines the creative contributions of two inventive cyclists on different sides of the English Channel with great success.

The 'official' cycle route, known as the Avenue Verte, goes from the London Eye on the south bank of the Thames to Notre Dame Cathedral on the Île de la Cité in the Seine. It crosses the Channel by ferry between Newhaven and Dieppe, and it is between 247 and 287 miles (388 and 462 km) long.

But is there a better route? In England Chris Smith stepped up to the challenge, and in France Donald Hirsch. Between them they conceived a route which involved only 200 miles (322 km) of cycling, using the Newhaven-Dieppe ferry crossing. Not only is it shorter (if a little hillier) – it's through more attractive landscapes too.

With Newhaven lying directly south of London, the route Smith carved out heads unswervingly southwards towards the port. From the Tower of London it snakes out through the ancient port of Limehouse in East London and past the launch site of Isambard Kingdom Brunel's last big transatlantic ship, the SS *Great Eastern*, on the Isle of Dogs (not an island, despite the name). Once a centre of shipbuilding, this is now a high-rise zone of high finance.

Crossing the River Thames through the Greenwich Pedestrian Tunnel, you emerge in Greenwich,

TOP: A historic start at the Tower of London, originated by a Frenchman, William the Conqueror.

MIDDLE: Lewes in East Sussex.

RIGHT: Cottages in Rodmell village.

OPPOSITE: It's a four-hour ferry crossing from Newhaven.

BOTTOM: If you feel the need for contemporary art en route, Israeli sculptor Dani Karavan's *Axe Majeure*, 'an urban intervention between classicism and modernity' can be experienced in Cergy-Pontoise.

BELOW: Neufchâtel-en-Bray.

BELOW RIGHT: The boating lake at Bois de Boulogne.

the heart of Britain's historic naval supremacy. The Greenwich Meridian is here, of course, showing 0° of longitude. The old tea clipper the *Cutty Sark* is berthed here too, and the National Maritime Museum is a treasure house of nautical history.

The route makes its way south through rural Greenwich Park, Ladywell Fields and South Norwood Country Park, sharing its path at times with the Green London Way, a 105-mile (170-km) circular trail around the city. On the North Downs north of Oxted it passes by the 350-year-old Outwood Windmill.

At East Grinstead you'll find the northern terminus of the celebrated Bluebell heritage steam railway, which enhances the landscape as it puffs (very slowly) across the South Downs. While Smith's route continues south from here, the

Avenue Verte heads unexpectedly east towards Tunbridge Wells, then south to Hailsham before approaching Newhaven from the south-east. Lewes, the principal town of the South Downs and next on Smith's route, has a lot to offer – a castle, a priory, and the former home of Anne of Cleves (one of Henry VIII's six wives). In the village of Rodmell between Lewes and Newhaven is the home of the authors Leonard and Virginia Woolf. From Newhaven, ferries depart for Dieppe, but before you rush through customs, visit Newhaven Fort at the mouth of the River Ouse, which has defended the estuary since 1548.

On the French side of *La Manche* (you wouldn't expect them to call it the *English* Channel) Donald Hirsch follows the Avenue Verte to begin with, along an old railway line through the ancient Pays de Bray. This is dairy country and the

route leads to Neufchâtel-en-Bray, famous for its sharp, salty cheese made the same way since the seventh century.

The path continues to Forges-les-Eaux. As its name suggests, Forges was known as a centre of iron production as early as the Roman era; the waters, les Eaux, refer to its popularity since the sixteenth century as a spa town. Forges, and Gournay-en-Bray a little closer to Paris, both sent knights to fight with William the Conqueror at the Battle of Hastings (not that far from Newhaven) and were rewarded with land in England.

After Gournay, Hirsch and the Avenue Verte diverge. The latter has two options, both indirect – south towards Giverny or west through Clermont. Hirsch ploughs resolutely onwards south-east straight towards Paris, through the Vexin Français Regional Nature Park. All three paths cross again in Cergy, from where it is a relatively short ride into Paris. The Avenue approaches the city from the north, through

busy St Denis (burial place of almost every French king between the tenth and eighteenth centuries); Donald Hirsch's route passes through the Bois de Boulogne to the south, and only uses city roads (and quiet ones at that) when it gets to within a couple of kilometres of the Eiffel Tower.

The Avenue Verte has several advantages over the Smith-Hirsch way: it is flatter, and signposted, and because it is officially recognized, it is designed around existing cycling infrastructure. The Smith-Hirsch, being unofficial, has no signage and is not afraid to use occasional back roads shared with motor traffic. Detailed maps and directions for it are available online, and it is shorter and prettier. You could do it in a few days, or you could spend a week or two enjoying the sights along the way. A return journey between Paris and London is possible by Eurostar train. Alternatively, you may continue beyond Paris for further French fields, such as the beautiful Veloscenic route from the capital to Mont St Michel.

BELOW LEFT: There's no missing the garish signposting of the Avenue Verte.

BELOW: From one iconic city landmark to another, you can easily spot the cycling tourists from the locals in Paris – they have cycle helmets.

Molesworth Muster Trail

New Zealand

Length: 207 km, 129 miles
Start: Blenheim
Finish: Hanmer Springs
Highlights: SS *Waverley*, Awatere Valley, Tapuae-o-Uenuku, Molesworth Cobb Cottage, Acheron Valley, Acheron Homestead, Clarence River, Jollies Pass, Ferry Bridge

Molesworth Muster Station is the largest farm in New Zealand, over 180,000 hectares in size. A 3- to 5-day trail along it takes you from the Wairau River to the Waiau River, deep into the area's geological past in a land explored by both Maori and European settlers.

This is a route that shows a part of New Zealand little changed from when the first settlers explored it. Apart from a short, sharp descent near the southern end of the route, it is a gentle ride on unsurfaced tracks along valley floors. It moves from the vineyards of Blenheim across the wild watershed between the regions of Marlborough and Canterbury to the alpine surroundings of Hanmer Springs.

Marlborough takes its name from the first Duke of Marlborough, a British military hero who in 1704 won the Battle of Blenheim, from which the starting point of this trail gets its name. Before then it was known to European settlers as Beaverton. Today it is known for producing the world's finest Sauvignon Blanc, but long before the immigrant Europeans arrived, Maoris had settled the area and dug over 18 km of irrigation channels to fertilize the land, drawing water from the Wairau and its tributary the Opawa.

Blenheim sits on a tight bend of the latter where it is joined by the Taylor River, and today the fertile land is occupied by vineyards producing the Sauvignon Blanc grape for which it has become famous. Nearby, the rivers all meet on the Pacific Coast and form the Big Lagoon, where the rusting hulk of the SS *Waverley* is a picturesque sight. She carried passengers and freight around the New Zealand coast for 45 years before being stranded here by a flood tide in 1928.

The Molesworth Trail leaves Blenheim on State Highway 1 heading south for 20 km, with one short climb as it switches from the Opawa Valley to the Awatere. At a crossroads before Seddon, it turns right onto the Awatere Valley Road, and follows the river upstream for the next 100 km. The first 60 km are surfaced and the landscape green and wooded; this road serves several vineyards along the way.

The road changes abruptly to dust and its character changes too. This is now farming country, and at times the track veers into the hills to avoid a steep-sided section of the valley below. It passes stations like Awapiri and the Campden Cookshop, which sprung up originally as sleeping huts for men driving livestock over this isolated route.

TOP: A storm brewing over the Kaikoura Mountains in the Upper Awatere Valley.

ABOVE: The trail near Molesworth Station.

OPPOSITE: A familiar sight in New Zealand – rows of vines in the Wairau Valley at Blenheim.

The valley cuts through the Inland Kaikoura mountains, one of a pair of parallel ranges. After the Campden Cookshop the road passes the foothills of their highest peak, Tapuae-o-Uenuku (2,885 metres/9,465 ft), 'footprint of the rainbow', to the south. The Kaikoura mountains and valleys were formed by the Marlborough geological fault system, which is still active – Blenheim still experiences several earthquakes a year. The braided streams of the river and its tributaries are an indication that water levels can change dramatically, especially during the winter melt.

As the track approaches Molesworth Station it starts to climb away from the valley again, and a lookout rock close to the road is a great place to look back on where you've come from. Molesworth Station itself lies in the valley below, and you can see an original accommodation house there, Molesworth Cobb Cottage, built in 1866. Fertilized by animal dung, this part of the valley is noticeably greener than others. But here

ABOVE: Looking across the Clarence River valley.

LEFT: Cyclists on the Molesworth Road near Acheron Station.

the trail turns away for good from the Awatere Valley, following a wooded stream up to the highest point of the route as it crosses over into the Acheron Valley.

A pleasant descent takes the track down to join another as it crosses the river, and 2.5 km further on, a gate across the road marks the western extent of the Molesworth Station. Beyond it the land belongs to the Muller Station, and from it a track leads deep into the mountains alongside the Saxon River to a remote shelter, the Saxon Hut, in the Raglan Mountains to the north. The Molesworth Trail continues along the Acheron, crossing the Saxon and descending to a broad flat plain. There's an airstrip here, and one at Molesworth too, should you need one.

At the point where the Severn River joins the Acheron there's another shelter hut. The Acheron is larger now, fed by tributary streams from various wooded valleys. As you cross from Marlborough into Canterbury, the river is itself swallowed up by the Clarence. This mighty river separates the Inland Kaikoura range from the Seaward Kaikoura.

The trail follows the Clarence upstream, passing the Acheron Homestead, another former drovers' shelter. At a junction of three dusty roads, the route leaves the Clarence and strikes south across the Jollies Pass Road. There's a little climbing to be done here, but from the summit it's a grand freewheel down for the final 6 km into Hanmer Springs. Although strictly speaking the route ends here, the extra 8 km to Ferry Bridge over the Waiau River to the south is worthwhile. It has been the main access to the town since 1887, a delicate metal structure across a deep narrow gorge.

Hot springs were discovered in Hanmer in 1859. For 20 years they were no more than a natural pool, with some steps into it and a wooden shed in which to change. The government of the day built a more formal bathhouse in 1884, and in 2010 it was extended to include a lazy river and other more modern features.

Among Hanmer's other attractions are helicopter rides over the terrain through which the Molesworth Muster Trail runs; and in winter, when the trail is closed, there are two ski areas. In streets immediately surrounding the spa complex there are innumerable bars and restaurants in which to relive the trail you've just completed.

RIGHT: Take time out from the dust and gravel and enjoy the thermal springs at Hanmer Springs.

BELOW: Waiau Ferry Bridge over the Waiau River near Hamner Springs.

Mont Ventoux

France

Length: 137 km, 85 miles
Start/Finish: Bédoin, Malaucène or Sault
Highlights: The villages, Chalet Reynard, the summit – it's all about the ride

Nicknamed 'Le Géant de Provence', the Giant of Provence, Mont Ventoux towers over the surrounding countryside. At 1,912 metres (6,273 ft) it's the only mountain of its size in the area, and the scene of the most challenging and venerated of all stages in the Tour de France.

Tours have been won and lives lost on the gruelling slopes of Mont Ventoux. Belgian legend Eddy Merckx had to be given oxygen after winning a stage there in 1972. In 1967 British rider Tom Simpson died when he insisted on getting back on his bike after collapsing from exhaustion. A granite memorial to him stands within sight of the summit. And in 2013 British cyclist Chris Froome won the stage, an early indication that he was about to snatch the first of his four Tour de France victories.

There are three different climbs to the top of Mont Ventoux, each between 21 and 25 km. One is usually enough for anyone, and to ascend all three in a day involves a round trip of 137 km. Anyone who completes the triple is entitled, for a fee, to join Le Club des Cinglés du Mont Ventoux, the Mont Ventoux Crazies Club, where you will be in the company of around 13,000 other lunatics.

Of the three individual routes, the classic climb begins at the village of Bédoin to the west of Ventoux. This road rises 1,610 metres (5,282 ft) over 21 km, much of it on constant, punishing gradients of 9–10%.

North of Bédoin and slightly higher on the foothills of Ventoux lies the village of Malaucène, from which a second route climbs 1,570 metres (5,151 ft) over a similar distance. Although less busy than the Bédoin ascent, it has a much more variable gradient, presenting a greater challenge to your stamina and strength. There are stretches of up to 15% and others of only 5–6%.

To the east of the Giant of Provence the third route begins at Sault. This, highest of the three starts, is a little longer at 26 km; but from Sault you only have to climb 1,220 metres (4,003 ft) to the summit, on a generally gentler incline.

The Sault and Bédoin routes meet at the Chalet Reynard, a café from where they share a road to the top. Chalet Reynard, originally a bad-weather refuge and now next to a small ski and MTB area, has a free tap to refill your water bottles. You'll be glad of it. Over the last 2 km you will be climbing at 10%: you are going to work up a thirst.

TOP: Lavender fields below the village of Sault.

ABOVE: Cyclists pay their respects at the Tom Simpson memorial, close to the summit of Ventoux.

OPPOSITE: Still below the tree line on the ascent of Ventoux.

Mount Desert Island's Scenic Trails

Maine, USA

Length: 80.5 miles, 130 km
Start/Finish: Bar Harbor
Highlights: Bar Harbor, Cadillac Mountain, Sand Beach, Eagle Lake, Chasm Brook Bridge, Somes Sound, Echo Lake, Bass Harbor Head Lighthouse

In former times a battleground, a rural idyll and a playground for the wealthy, Mount Desert Island is something of a paradise for the cyclist. Incorporating roads built a century ago for the sole use of hikers and bikers, there's an almost infinite variety of looping trails.

Mount Desert Island, known locally by its initials MDI, is the second largest island on the eastern seaboard of the US (after Long Island). It's joined to Trenton on mainland Maine by a bridge and causeway across the Mount Desert Narrows, and to Nova Scotia by a ferry from the island's main settlement, Bar Harbor.

To the uninitiated the island's name is confusing. It is the island of Mount Desert, not the mountain of Desert Island. The barren summit of Cadillac Mountain, the island's highest point, seemed like a desert to its 1603 European discoverer Samuel de Champlain, in comparison to the woodland covering most of the rest of the island.

OPPOSITE: The very popular Beehive Lagoon and beach.

ABOVE RIGHT: Schooner Head Road in Acadia National Park.

RIGHT: Experiencing the aural sensation of Thunder Hole in Acadia National Park.

Geologically the island consists of a series of ridges running north to south with lakes between them – principally Seal Cove Pond, Long Pond, Jordan Pond and Eagle Lake, and the saltwater inlet Somes Sound which nearly bisects the island. The highest land, including Cadillac Mountain, is in the eastern half of Mount Desert Island. To the native Wabanaki people it was known as Pemetic, 'the sloping land'; but don't be alarmed cyclists: the only really sustained, punishing climb is the ascent of Cadillac Mountain itself.

Just 270 miles from Quebec City, MDI often found itself on the front line of the battle for territory between French Acadia and New England. After the American War of Independence MDI's British owner Francis Bernard was evicted, and his son John (who had fought for the revolutionaries) was granted half the island. The other half went to the granddaughter of an earlier French owner of the island, Antoine de la Mothe Cadillac (better known as the founder of the city of Detroit). Cadillac Mountain is named after him.

In the nineteenth century the island became popular with artists who didn't mind the basic living conditions they could afford there. Soon, paintings of the romantic coastal landscape caught the attention of wealthy New York patrons who began to visit the island; by 1880 there were 30 hotels on Mount Desert Island, and the richest families in America were building summer

BELOW: Carriage Road Bridge near Bubble Rock in Acadia National Park.

BOTTOM: A footbridge restored by the Mount Desert Island Historic Society in Somesville

retreats there – Astor, Vanderbilt, Rockefeller and others – with fine landscaped grounds designed by the great designer Beatrix Farrand.

Other incomers chose to settle permanently on the island and campaigned to preserve its rural character. It became a National Park in 1919, and John D. Rockefeller Jr. gave large areas of land to the Park. He also built around 50 miles of traffic-free roads with artfully placed rustic stone bridges, for the pleasure of walkers and cyclists in summer and cross-country skiers in winter. These form the basis of many of the trails on the island today – but do be aware that most of the island's other roads are shared with cars.

There are several large settlements on MDI, composed of many smaller villages; any of them makes a good base from which to explore the island, which is only 16 miles long and at most 14 miles wide. It's an island to be enjoyed at your leisure, but if you want to give yourself a

challenge, there's a testing 80-mile circuit which covers both MDI's interior and almost the entire coastline. Parts of this route are free from traffic.

It starts in Bar Harbor on the east coast and tackles the toughest part out of the route immediately – the ascent of Cadillac Mountain. Starting at sea level the route climbs 1,530 ft (466 metres) to the summit in just over six miles, with gradients of up to 12%. The descent is by the same road, so you won't miss anything but the magnificent view and the freewheel descent if you decide to skip this leg of the journey. From the bottom, the route follows the coastline in a clockwise direction.

There are trailheads aplenty along the way, and at Schooner Head Overlook a chance to get up close and personal with the water's rocky edge before the road drops gently down past Beehive Lagoon to the white arc of Sand Beach. Beyond the beach there's dramatic Thunder Hole, where the wind drives the waves onshore; and after the village of Otter Creek the trail leaves the tarmac road for some of Rockefeller's crushed-stone carriageways. It makes an optional loop around the testing Triad Pass before following Hunters Brook upstream to Eagle Lake, the largest of the island's inland waters.

Still off-tarmac the route travels three-quarters of the way around the Lake before striking off around Sargent Peak, crossing Rockefeller's Chasm Brook Bridge on its way to rejoining the public road on the eastern side of Somes Sound, the only fjord in the Eastern States. The Sound and the village of Somesville at its head are named after Abraham Somes, one of the settlers introduced by British owner Francis Bernard to the island.

From Somesville you can take a shortcut northwards to Eden Village, and follow the coast back to Bar Harbor, or continue south on the western side of the Sound. The road climbs past (usually) tranquil Echo Lake to Southwest Harbor and on, around Bass Harbor Head, to Tremont. The Head is the most southerly point of MDI, and picturesque Bass Harbor Head Lighthouse clings halfway up a cliff here.

Beyond Tremont the route uses minor roads wherever possible to stick as close as it can to the gentle western coast of the island, heading north and then eastwards along the Mount Desert Narrows back to the starting point of Bar Harbor.

MDI's population of a little over 10,000 permanent residents is swelled each year by around 3.5 million visitors. The secret of the island's unspoilt character is out, but it is still possible, especially by bicycle, to find plenty of moments of quiet beauty throughout this genteel place.

RIGHT: Southwest Harbor, where you can see the Cranberries: Great Cranberry Island and Little Cranberry Island.

BELOW: The Bass Harbor Head Lighthouse.

Mount Evans Scenic Byway

Colorado, USA

Length: 27.9 miles, 45 km
Start: Idaho Springs
Finish: The summit
Highlights: Argo Gold Mine, Charlie Taylor Water Wheel, Echo Lake, Summit Lake, Crest House, Meyer-Womble Observatory, views

The Mount Evans Scenic Byway makes it possible to walk, pedal or drive to within a few feet of the mountain top on immaculately laid tarmac with gradients averaging only 4.7%. But if you think this is mountaineering for softies, think again.

Mount Evans isn't the highest mountain in Colorado or even the highest mountain in the Front Range, of which it forms a part. But it dominates the Denver skyline, and on a clear day it can be seen from a hundred miles away.

The Byway was completed in 1930 as part of a project by the Denver Mountain Parks authorities to link all their properties by road. At less than 28 miles, it's not challenging in length for a moderately fit cyclist. The challenge is the altitude, and the change in altitude from bottom to top. The starting point in Idaho Springs is already a lofty 7,526 ft (2,294 metres) above sea level, a height at which oxygen is already significantly scarcer. But from there cyclists must almost double their altitude: Mount Evans stands 14,130 ft (4,307 metres) tall. It's a brutal workout for the heart and lungs.

And it's not just the effort that takes its toll. The prevailing wind is from the south-west, and the road approaches the mountain from the north-east. The average annual temperature in the Springs is 43.4°F (6.3°C): at the summit it's 18°F (-8°C). On windy days the air temperature can halve the moment you break cover above the tree level, a little over halfway through the climb. By a cruel twist of fate, this stretch of the route is also the steepest, at up to 10%.

The route was designed specifically to open up magnificent vistas to those travelling on it. Beyond Echo Lake the road is closed in winter, but in the summer it clings to the unguarded flanks of Rogers Peak and Mount Warren, and climbs on past Summit Lake. In the final four-mile assault on the summit there are no fewer than thirteen hairpin bends. In the annual Mount Evans Hill Climb, cyclists *race* up this and the rest of the Byway, the highest paved road in the US. At the top there are the ruins of Crest House, a restaurant and gift shop which burnt down in 1979, and which kept oxygen on hand for visitors suffering from altitude sickness. Behind it is the Meyer-Womble Observatory, once the world's highest. Mount Evans has been a popular choice for high-altitude scientific studies by athletes and physicists. By the time you get there you'll have made your own scientific study of the effects of the climb on your body. You may be exhausted, but you are only 1,640 ft (500 metres) lower than the highest mountain in the Swiss Alps.

OPPOSITE: Doing Mount Evans the hard way, on a unicycle.

BELOW LEFT: The Argo Gold Mine in Idaho Springs.

BOTTOM LEFT: Echo Lake.

BELOW: Local wildlife includes *Oreamnos americanus* – or the mountain goat.

Munda Biddi Trail

Western Australia

Length: 1,000 km, 621 miles
Start: Mundaring
Finish: Albany
Highlights: Dwellingup, Donnelly River Village, Pemberton, Northcliffe, Yirra Kartta, Valley of Giants, Torndirrup National Park

Munda Biddi means 'trail through the forest'. Here is an MTB trail across wild, unspoilt south-western Australia where you may go for up to 100 km between traces of civilization. It's an adventure!

The trail runs inland and more or less parallel to the south-western corner of Australia, echoing but almost never overlapping the long-distance Bibbulmun Track, a walking trail to Albany on the south coast from Perth. The Munda Biddi starts near the Kalamunda suburb in Mundaring; but while the Bibbulmun crosses the Darling Mountain Range, the Munda Biddi is a merely hilly trail with the occasional short, steep incline. It claims to be the longest unbroken off-road route in the world, and it is almost entirely unpaved. Nothing less than a mountain bike, preferably with fat tyres, will do for this trail over mud, gravel and tree roots.

Although it passes through towns every 50–100 km, it is otherwise a fairly unsupported route. There are signs, but you should not rely solely on them for finding your way. A set of nine official maps covers the whole trail. There are occasional, well-equipped free campsites along the way, but you should plan carefully for supplies and accommodation. Avoid riding the Munda Biddi in high summer when the heat can be intense and the risk of bushfires high.

A sign in Mundaring's community sculpture park marks the northern terminus of the Munda Biddi. The trail heads south through Beelu National Park, following the Helena River upstream. Beelu means 'river', and refers to the local aboriginal people whose territory was defined by the Helena, Swan and Canning rivers. The route is hilly as it transfers from the Helena to the Canning Valley and then the Wungong on its way to Jarrahdale.

Jarrahdale grew up around the state's first venture into timber-milling in the nineteenth century, and today there are many historical traces of the industry in the town. There is also evidence of its brief boomtime as a mining town for nearby deposits of bauxite in the mid-twentieth century; and there's a welcome bar and general store for hungry, thirsty travellers.

Dwellingup, the next town to the south of Jarrahdale, has rather more facilities, and it's one of the few meeting points of the Munda Biddi and Bibbulmun Trails. It was another timber, town and nowadays it's a centre for outdoor activities including MTB trailing and white-water rafting. One end of the 32-km-long Hotham Valley steam heritage railway is here. Dwellingup was completely rebuilt after Western Australia's worst

OPPOSITE: A flooded ford across the Murray River in the Lane Poole Reserve.

BELOW: Come prepared if you're going to tackle the longest continuous off-road trail in the world.

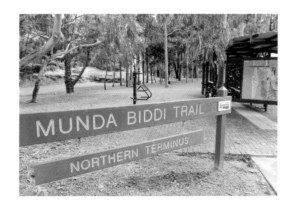

bushfire in 1961, when 132 homes were burnt to the ground. Nanga and its timber mill further south suffered the same fate in the flames and were abandoned afterwards. The site of that town is now a campsite on the Munda Biddi trail.

Beyond Nanga there are some popular waterfalls, but between there and the Logue Brook dam the trail gets tougher. You can bypass the worst of this section with a short diversion. The trail continues through rich forestry. One of the main species of tree that brought the area its early wealth was the jarrah, a member of the eucalyptus family. Its tall, straight trunk was valued for its hardness, and many early roads were made of jarrah beams covered in asphalt. Bees feed on its white flowers to make a rich, dark honey.

ABOVE: The HQ of Nannup Historical Society. In the town, there is a statue of Marinko Tomas, the first Western Australian serviceman killed in the Vietnam War (1966).

RIGHT: Pemberton's famous Gloucester Tree.

Surrounded by dense jarrah forest and at the meeting of two rivers is one of the largest towns on the trail, Collie. Among other attractions, the town has an underground mining museum, a steam locomotive collection and a bike shop. Collie is a mining town, once notoriously dirty with coal dust but now a seasoned winner of the Australia-wide Tidy Town competition.

From Collie the trail turns westwards to skirt around the huge Wellington reservoir, on some of the toughest terrain of the route. It emerges

briefly from forestry to farming land on its way to the small settlement of Boyerup, where there are stores and a bar. Beyond Boyerup, Jarrahwood was named after the Jarrah Wood and Sawmills Company which operated here; it once had shops, schools, a hospital, a post office and even a railway service on a line built by the company. After the mill's closure in 1982 the population fell to just 20. There's nothing here at all except a Community House, where you can get a bed for the night.

Nannup, next on the trail, has fared better. It still has a working mill and the area has also diversified into vineyards. The Nannup Music Festival takes place every March. Further along the trail in the village of Donnelly River, the mill has closed but the workers' cottages are now holiday homes. The general store has a café and there's a large population of very tame emus and kangaroos. This is the halfway point on the Munda Biddi Trail.

From Donnelly River, the route continues through forests of jarrah and karri (another eucalyptus species) before emerging into open farmland around Manjimup. Manjimup's climate has made it a surprisingly diverse centre of agriculture. Here they grow vines, fruits and vegetables, and the town once had a thriving tobacco industry. It is a major producer of black truffles, and experts are now experimenting with green tea varieties because the climate is similar to that of Japan's Shizuoka tea-growing region. The Pink Lady apple variety was created here.

The trail from Manjimup curls clockwise through the tiny settlement of Quinninup (the '-up' placename element so common along this trail means 'meeting place') to Pemberton, another timber town which has successfully embraced tourism. It is a centre for outdoor sports including canoeing and hiking. The Bibbulmun Trail passes through the town, which, like Dwellingup, has a heritage steam railway. In the forests surrounding

it you can climb 60-metre-high (197-ft) karri trees on specially placed pegs around their trunks. Pemberton has a bank and a hospital.

Many of the areas through which the Munda Biddi Trail passes were allocated to participants in the Group Settlement Scheme after World War I. A similar scheme for soldiers had been set up as early as 1915 to assist their re-entry into civilian life, and in the economic depression of the 1920s the Western Australia government saw an opportunity to encourage civilians to open up new tracts of land for agriculture, especially dairy farming. The British Government saw this as a useful way of reducing the United Kingdom's post-war unemployment, and around 6,000 people relocated to Western Australia, attracted by the scheme's incentives.

Most of the areas exploited by the scheme centred on existing townships. Northcliffe, south of Pemberton, is the only town specifically created by the Group Settlement Scheme. The town was named after Lord Northcliffe, head of

LEFT: Museum piece – an engine formerly belonging to the State Saw Mills slowly rusting in Pemberton.

BELOW: Giant Karri trees up to 90 metres (295 ft) tall near Northcliffe.

TOP: Elephant Cove, Denmark.

ABOVE: A tree-lined avenue to match Northern Ireland's famous Dark Hedges.

LEFT: Valley of the Giants tree-top walk near Walpole-Nornalup.

the Propaganda Bureau in London during the war and owner of *The Times* newspaper, which actively promoted the scheme through its pages. The scheme was largely successful; 40,000 hectares were opened up to a dairy industry which thrives today, although many of the immigrant settlers were poorly equipped with the skills and resilience required of pioneers. Northcliffe, still a dairy town today, has a museum dedicated to those pioneers. In forests nearby there is Understory, a sculpture trail by 40 artists.

Between Northcliffe and Walpole, where the trail at last reaches the coast on the Nornalup Inlet, Yirra Kartta is a massive granite outcrop sacred to the original population of the area. There is a camp site nearby and the spirituality of the place is tangible. Walpole serves a wide rural community with basic facilities; and from the town there are cruises around the inlet. Near the trail to the east of Walpole, the Valley of Giants tree-top walk is a series of steel bridges through the canopy of the forest, giving a very different perspective on the habitat through which the trail has passed.

The trail runs along the coast as it approaches the sizeable town of Denmark on Wilson Inlet. Denmark was founded by a Dutchman and named after an Englishman, Alexander Denmark. It was a beneficiary of the Group Settlement Scheme and became a holiday destination for US troops based at nearby Albany during World War II. Now its population rises dramatically during the tourist season.

The short ride from Denmark to Albany passes near West Cape Howe, the most southerly point of mainland Western Australia. Albany, the end of the trail, is the oldest permanent settlement in the state and now a large city and port. Its history includes convicts and whale hunters, and in 1914 many ANZAC soldiers departed from here for the disastrous Gallipoli campaign from which so few returned.

Today whaling has given way to whale-watching. Across the harbour from the city, Torndirrup National Park has a notoriously rugged coastline from which giant waves have been known to sweep the unwary into the sea. There are plenty of safe sandy beaches nearby, however, and in the city itself many colonial buildings survive. There is plenty to see and do in Albany and it's worth spending a few days here while you recover from and reflect on the 1,000-km 'trail through the forest' behind you.

TOP: *Cheynes IV* whaling ship berthed at Whale World Museum at Frenchman Bay, Albany.

ABOVE: York Street in Albany.

North Sea Cycle Route

Norway, Sweden, Denmark, Germany, The Netherlands, Belgium, Great Britain

Length: 5,900 km, 3,666 miles
Start: Bergen
Finish: Unst
Highlights: Preikestolen, Gothenburg, Hvide Sande, Tipperne Peninsula, Heligoland, Bruges, Lincoln, Edinburgh, St Andrews, Johnshaven, John O'Groats, Ring of Brodgar, Lerwick, Muckle Flugga

Not many bike trails take you through seven countries, or on ten sea ferries. The giant horseshoe-shaped North Sea Cycle Route takes you from coast to coast – to coast, to coast, to coast …

The European Union was established as a means of preventing war between nations through the medium of trade. The result has been an equalization of standards and practices across member states, even if some are questioning the extent to which this results in a loss of cultural individuality. But the vision of a United Europe has resulted in one undeniable benefit, the creation of nearly 20 magnificent long-distance cycle trails.

Under the EuroVelo banner these include EV2, the Capitals Route from Dublin to Moscow; EV3, the Pilgrims Route; and EV13, the Iron Curtain Trail. Sections of the latter two are included in this book. There are also EuroVelo routes along a number of coastlines – the Atlantic (EV1), the Mediterranean (EV8) and the Baltic (EV10). These are not light undertakings and demand a high degree of planning and coordination. And time.

EV12 is the North Sea Cycle Route. It runs along almost every inch of shore of the North Sea between Great Britain, Northern Europe and Scandinavia. At around 5,900 km in length it's unlikely that you'll have time to complete it all in a single journey – it could take two to three months. But it will be scarcely less of an achievement to tackle it section by section over a few years.

The EuroVelo routes are a relatively new initiative and those undertaking them should be aware that parts of them are better established than others. At best they run on dedicated cycle paths with full EuroVelo signposting. Other sections simply adopt national cycle trails and signage. Some stages are little more than outline proposals, on local paths and roads which have not yet been agreed on as the final route of the Route.

So it is, for example, with the opening stretch of the North Sea Cycle Route. It begins in Bergen, Norway, and follows the coast to the border with Sweden at Svinesund. The whole Norwegian section has yet to be finalized within EV12, but the roads and paths are part of Norwegian Cycle Route 1 and they take you through some magnificent coastal scenery. Early on it hops from island to island, partly on bridges and partly on three ferry crossings. There are towering cliffs on this coastline too, including the popular tourist spot the Preikestolen, the 'Preacher's Pulpit', a 600-metre-high (1,969 ft) natural stone platform jutting out over the Lysefjord near Stavanger.

TOP: Fish market in front of the Domkirken (cathedral), Bergen.

ABOVE: Crossing the river Haa in Norway.

OPPOSITE: The knee-trembling Pulpit Rock at Lysefjord, Norway.

Another ferry crosses the Outer Oslofjord. The Norwegian capital is about 65 km to the north, but the main route turns south and crosses into Sweden. As far as Gothenburg (Göteborg) it is classified as 'under development' – that is, it has been finalized and some necessary upgrading is being undertaken. Gothenburg is Sweden's second largest city, one of the great historical ports of the Old World. Its shipping wealth has created a city of rich architectural and cultural delights.

From Gothenburg onwards, and for the rest of the trail, the route is complete, although some stretches are still not fully signposted as EV12 – beyond Göteborg, for example, it is Swedish National Route 1. North of Malmö it crosses the Kattegat, the stretch of water linking the North and Baltic Seas, and follows Denmark's peninsular coastline in an anticlockwise direction. Denmark has over 11,000 km of dedicated cycle lanes and paths, and all relatively flat compared to the rest of Scandinavia.

The North Sea Route follows Danish National Routes 5 and 1 around the coast, passing through the fishing harbour of Hvide Sande in the west. Hvide Sande sits on a long spit of sand dunes at a point where a canal has been dug through to connect the sea to the large lagoon behind it – Ringkøbing Fjord. Nearby, the Tipperne Peninsula, which juts into the fjord, is the largest bird reserve in Europe, a vital stopover for migratory species. It was created from sand in storms only a few hundred years ago and is still growing.

The Route crosses the Vidå inlet to enter Germany at the village of Rosenkranz and continues on German National Cycle Route 1. From several points along this north-western shore of Germany ferries depart for Heligoland, about 70 km offshore and worth the detour. Pretty houses and beaches surround an island with a chequered history. Originally Danish, it passed to Britain for most of the nineteenth century, during which time a visitor to the island wrote the lyrics for the German national anthem. Since 1890 it has been a German possession but retains a language (Heligolandic) and atmosphere all its own.

From Germany it's on through the Netherlands (with national routes LF10 and LF1) and Belgium (LF1). The Dutch section is described in detail elsewhere in this book. Set back slightly from

the Belgian coast, the charming city of Bruges is built on canals in the manner of Amsterdam. Its historic buildings reflect its Golden Age from the twelfth to the fifteenth century.

The route then reaches the French border, from which cyclists make their way to England. There the trail follows British National Cycle Route 1 for the rest of the way, picking it up at the busy international port of Harwich. The Mayflower sailed from here in 1620. If the coastal route doesn't always stick to the coast in England, it's only to introduce cyclists to some of the country's handsome cathedral cities – Norwich, Lincoln and Durham are all on the trail.

ABOVE: Hummerbuden, or lobster shacks, on Heligoland.

RIGHT: In Bruges, take a tourist boat around the canals; alternatively climb the 366 narrow steps of the towering Bruges Belfry.

Between Bridlington and Saltburn-by-the-Sea it passes through some of England's best-loved seaside resorts, including Scarborough and Whitby. The latter's connections with Dracula have made it a place of pilgrimage for goths, and further north, in Seahouses, they serve some of the freshest, finest fish and chips in the country.

Crossing into Scottish border territory near Berwick-upon-Tweed the route approaches

capital city Edinburgh, the self-styled Festival City. Here, at the right time of year, you can find a Festival of just about anything, from television to jazz, from books to science, from film to Hogmanay (the Scottish New Year). The original Edinburgh Festival and its much larger offspring the Edinburgh Fringe run throughout August and fill the city to bursting point with actors, dancers, comedians, people handing out flyers and their audiences.

From Edinburgh the trail leads to St Andrews, the home of golf, and on to the Angus coast, a rugged shore of small fishing villages like Johnshaven and Gardenstown, as well as the important northern cities of Aberdeen and Inverness. The population thins out dramatically in the Scottish Highlands north of Inverness. The North Sea Route eschews the extremely busy east coast road to head inland. It reaches the sea again on the Pentland Firth, whose powerful tidal currents make it one of the most dangerous stretches of water in the British Isles. At its

eastern end lies desolate John O'Groats, the most north-easterly place in mainland Britain.

But this is not the end of the North Sea Cycle Route. Ferries from here go further north to the archipelago of Orkney, an extraordinary landscape of small islands and prehistoric sites older than Stonehenge, with an atmosphere quite distinct from the rest of Scotland. From Orkney another ferry crosses the sea to Shetland, even closer to the Arctic Circle. Here, culturally, the people are closer to Norway than to Britain. The principle town, Lerwick, is only slightly further south than Bergen where the Route began.

And from it the trail goes further north still, by ferry to Yell and by another on to Unst, the most northerly of all the inhabited British Isles. Unst has flora and fauna unique in Britain and when you have cycled as far as you can go, to the northernmost tip of Hermanness Nature Reserve, you can see the rocky island of Muckle Flugga with its unmanned lighthouse; and beyond that,

ABOVE LEFT: A cast-iron Victorian lighthouse in Harwich, Essex.

TOP: Durham Cathedral overlooking the River Wear.

ABOVE: Work started on Lincoln Minster as far back as 1072.

a small low outcrop called Out Stack which is the absolute end of the country – once called 'the full stop at the end of Britain'.

The roads and paths throughout this trail are well maintained, and will suit any touring bike. The North Sea Cycle Route is a route of many countries and many cultures, which it draws together like one big seaside family through the simple pleasure of cycling. As they say in Norwegian, *god reise* – bon voyage.

TOP: The seafront in the seaside resort of Scarborough in North Yorkshire.

RIGHT: Crowds throng in the Royal Mile during the Edinburgh Festival. If you need accommodation in August, book a long way in advance.

FAR RIGHT TOP: John O'Groats, at the tip of mainland Scotland, doesn't have to be the end of the journey.

FAR RIGHT BOTTOM: Skara Brae, the well-preserved neolithic settlement on Orkney.

Oregon Coast

Oregon, USA

Length: 369 miles, 594 km
Start: Astoria, Oregon
Finish: Crescent City, California
Highlights: The bridges of Conde McCullough, Fort Astoria and Depoe Bay, the lighthouses of Yaquina Head and Bay, Cape Perpetua, Port Orford, the Wild Rivers Coast

Only in the last hundred years has the rugged Oregon coast been tamed for vehicle use. Steep cliffs and wide river estuaries made any road along it an engineering challenge. Now that it has been conquered it's yours to enjoy.

It's largely thanks to the engineering genius of Conde B. McCullough that a bike ride along the Oregon Coast is possible at all. Sliced through by countless rivers from the Cascade Mountains, the Oregon coast was a difficult road to travel, reliant on ferries across waters often swollen by the high rainfall of the region. Completed in 1926, the Oregon Coast Highway was built as part of historic US 101, which spans the Pacific Coast from Washington to California. In Oregon, McCullough's elegant bridges over six major rivers and seventeen others are the undoubted man-made highlights of the route. In the year following their completion, visitor numbers to Pacific Oregon rose by 72%.

The real star, however, is the unspoilt nature of the rocky, forested landscape which those bridges open up for the tourist. Thanks to progressive state legislation the entire seashore of Oregon is open to the public and environmentally protected by dozens of State Parks and National Nature Reserves.

The route has some steep gradients, but a fit cyclist can complete the run north to south in a week. A more average family of cyclists might want to take twice as long to enjoy some of the trip's delights. There's plenty of accommodation along the coast, but not many bicycle stores en route. Luckily, the way is all paved.

It starts in Astoria at the mouth of the Columbia River, which marks the boundary between Oregon and Washington. The river was considered too wide to bridge when Conde McCullough was at work and from 1926 a regular ferry made the crossing to Megler WA. In 1966, however, the Astoria-Megler Bridge was constructed, and remains the longest continuous truss in North America. It was the last section of Highway 101 from Olympia to Los Angeles to be completed.

Astoria is the oldest city in Oregon and 'the oldest permanent US settlement west of the Mississippi' (that's if you discount all the ones founded by the Spanish). Founded in 1811, Fort Astoria was a base for John Jacob Astor's American Fur Company and you can visit a replica of it today. Before that, explorers Meriwether Lewis and William Clark spent the winter of 1806–7 in a more modest log structure, now reconstructed to the west of the city in Lewis and Clark National

TOP: Nehalem Bay, Manzanita.

ABOVE: Depoe Bay has the world's narrowest natural harbour entrance, making it a very secure harbour.

OPPOSITE: Astoria-Megler Bridge spanning the Columbia River.

Historic Park. The pair also feature in murals of early Oregon history painted on the 1926 Astoria Column, from the top of whose 164 steps you get a view worth climbing for.

The coast itself is a mixture of rock and sand, high cliffs and quiet beaches, mountains and dunes. Nehalem Bay, formed by a barrier of built-up sand where the Pacific tide and the Nehalem River collide, is typical of this rugged coastal geography. The road encounters numerous small communities situated on estuaries, established to take advantage of local natural resources.

At Depoe Bay further south, one of McCullough's bridges spans the narrow rocky passage that leads to the town's tiny harbour. A pod of gray whales lives offshore for ten months of the year, making this the whale-watching capital of Oregon – but migrating whales and lingering sea lions are a common sight almost anywhere along the state's coast.

ABOVE: Cook's Chasm near Yachats.

RIGHT: Coos Bay, a city of 16,000 souls, lies on the Coos River in Coos County.

On Yaquina Head, formerly known as Cape Foulweather, stands Oregon's tallest lighthouse, made in Paris and dispatched to Yaquina in 1868. There's then a five-mile-long beach between here and Yaquina Bay Lighthouse, Oregon's last surviving wooden light. Beside it at the village of Newport, another McCullough bridge crosses the Yaquina River.

If you like your coast battered by wind and tide, Cape Perpetua has much to offer. The rocky shore at its base has features from which the sea explodes dramatically: Devil's Churn, Spouting Horn, Cook's Chasm and Thor's Well are all worthy of a visit. On a clear day, the tree-covered headland, 800 ft (244 metres) high, offers a view of 70 miles of Oregon's coastline, 35 miles in either direction. A trail leads to a 600-year-old spruce, survivor of countless storms.

Coos Bay is the largest city on the Oregon Coast. The first European settlers here were mariners shipwrecked on the *Captain Lincoln* in 1852, who struggled to shore and set up Camp Castaway. Although other pioneers came to the area, the town remained largely cut off save for a wagon road, until the arrival of the railroad in 1916. The completion of Conde McCullough's bridge over the north bend of the bay finally joined the city to northern Oregon, and the bridge is now known as the McCullough Memorial Bridge.

After Coos Bay the communities are less frequent, the coast more rugged. This final stretch of Oregon coastline is known as the Wild Rivers Coast. There are sea stacks at Bandon, and at pretty Port Orford, where fishing boats are lifted out of the shallow harbour every day to protect them from tidal surges and storms.

Gold Beach, named not for the colour of the sand but for the precious metal once found in it, has another McCullough bridge and one of the last two mail boats in the US postal system, serving upstream communities on the Rogue River.

Soon after the town of Brookings on the Chetco River, Highway 101 crosses the border into the Golden State, California. At Pelican Bay, small islands offshore shield a deserted beach from the worst the Pacific can throw at it. The first centre of Californian population is Crescent City, named after the long curving arc of sand at the ocean's edge. You're not in Oregon any more, but if you want to continue southwards, the Redwood Highway and the classic Californian Pacific Coast Highway await your pleasure.

ABOVE: Sea stacks at Bandon.

RIGHT: Crab pots stacked on the quay in Port Orford.

Otago Central Rail Trail

New Zealand

Length: 152 km, 94 miles
Start: Clyde
Finish: Middlemarch
Highlights: Ophir, Poolburn Gorge, Oturehua, Wedderburn Goods Shed, Ranfurly, Waipiata Green Bridge, Taieri Gorge Railway

New Zealand's pioneering first off-road leisure cycle route was formally opened in 2000. Since then its popularity has steadily increased, and now some 15,000 cyclists enjoy it each year, reaching a peak in the late summer months of March and April.

The Otago Central Branch Railway originally ran from Dunedin on the east coast of South Island, to Cromwell in the centre of the island. It was constructed between 1877 and 1921 to serve miners and gold prospectors in the hills of the North Rough Ridge, the island's spine.

It was closed down in 1990 after it had been used to carry the materials for the Clyde Dam project. A short section at the Dunedin end was retained, but elsewhere the track was lifted. Even before it was officially opened it had become a popular walking and cycling route.

There had been some 22 passenger stations along the closed section. The small local communities which they served now provide ample accommodation along the trail and plenty of refreshment stops of all kinds. Its gradients are gentle, as you'd expect from a railway bed,

and reasonably fit cycling families will be able to complete it in three or four days.

Most people join the trail at its western terminus, Clyde. The township, originally called Dunstan, was renamed in 1865 in homage to Baron Clyde, who had died in 1863. He was a military man who served the British Empire with distinction during the Crimean War and the Indian Mutiny. Today Clyde is a busy tourist town catering for both cyclists and oenologists drawn to the region's vineyards.

From Clyde the trail follows the Clutha River south-east to the larger town of Alexandra, which grew out of the Otago Goldrush of the 1860s. Today this is fruit-growing country – not only grapes but cherries, plums and other stone-fruits – and both Clyde and Alexandra have springtime blossom festivals. Here the trail crosses the Manuherikia River, a tributary of the Clutha, before turning north-east to follow it upstream.

At the settlement of Omakau there are several historic buildings, including an 1898 hotel and a former branch of the Bank of New Zealand.

TOP: Ophir Post Office – still open, but sending fewer telegrams these days.

ABOVE RIGHT: Cyclists on the Poolburn Viaduct.

RIGHT: Heading straight towards the Ida Range.

OPPOSITE: A bridge on the trail between Ophir and Lauder.

temple in Jerusalem. New Zealand's Ophir was thus named after the fabled King Solomon's mines in the hope of being as productive. There is evidence of the gold rush all along the Otago Central – not just in the historic buildings but in traces of the watercourses built to pan the dirt for gold.

Soon after Lauder, the track crosses the Manuherikia river one last time, on the high, handsome, but prosaically named Manuherikia Bridge No. 1 – the longest bridge on the trail. Soon afterwards it enters a stretch of tunnels and bridges around the deep, steep-sided Poolburn Gorge. You may spot the remains of the camp which housed the tunnellers.

The Poolburn is swollen by the Idaburn river, which the railway now follows upstream as it climbs to the highest point of the Otago Central. This is the settlement of Idaburn, at 617 metres (2,024 ft) a little under 500 metres (1,640 ft) higher than Clyde. On the way to the summit the village of Oturehua is worth exploring, with old mine workings and extraction equipment on display. Today the Ida Valley has reverted to grass, grazed by cattle and Merino lambs.

The descent from Idaburn is gentler than the ascent to it. The goods shed at Wedderburn is a national landmark, having been the subject of a famous painting by New Zealand artist Grahame Sydney. The next major town, Ranfurly – named after the governor of New Zealand at the time of construction – is noted for its Art Deco architecture, especially its striking milk bar.

TOP: Wedderburn's old landmark green shed.

ABOVE: Lovers of author George Eliot can't pass up the chance of a photo-op in Middlemarch, which still has working rails.

Opposite Omakau, across the river, lies Ophir and its 50 residents. It was home to over 1,000 at the height of the gold rush in the 1860s, hence the presence of a courthouse and police station left over from those lawless times.

In biblical history Ophir was where King Solomon acquired the gold with which he covered the

Grahame Sydney also immortalized Waipiata beyond Ranfurly. Waipiata has important road and rail bridges across the Taieri river, which is prone to flooding in the high Maniototo Plain. The Otago Central follows the bends of the Taieri at a safe distance for the rest of its journey. After passing through Prices Creek Tunnel you arrive at Hyde, where there's a memorial to a

sad piece of railway history. Twenty-one people died in the Hyde Railway Disaster of 1943 when an express passenger train left the rails in a cutting. It was New Zealand's worst rail disaster at the time.

Hyde sits at the northern end of the Rock and Pillar mountain range, on the western slopes of which the Taieri has its source. The range is unusually flat-topped and the upper surfaces are covered by the Great Moss Swamp. Look for the strange and permanent cloud formation above it, which locals call the Taieri Pet. The Rock and Pillar Range is one of only two homes of the rare Burgan Skink, a lizard first identified in the Burgan Stream which flows in the range.

The Otago Central Trail ends in Middlemarch, a small town whose population swells during the sheep-shearing season. The trail ends here because the old Otago Central Railway track still survives from here to Dunedin. It is now run as a heritage line, the Taieri Gorge Railway, and a journey through the gorge by train back to Dunedin makes a fitting end to this cycle through New Zealand's past and present.

ABOVE: Loganburn Reservoir, the Great Moss Swamp and, beyond them, the snow-capped Pillar Range.

RIGHT: The still extant rail line to Dunedin runs heritage trains through the Taieri Gorge.

P'tit Train du Nord

Quebec, Canada

Length: 200 km, 124 miles
Start: Mont-Laurier
Finish: Saint-Jérôme
Highlights: Mont-Laurier Rapids, Lac des Écorces and Lac Gauvin, La Maison du Cheminot at Labelle, Devil's River, Rivière du Nord, Sainte-Adèle station

What was once part of the Canadian Pacific Railway network is now a popular bicycle trail through the grandeur of the Laurentian Mountains. More people travel on it now than ever did by train.

Le P'tit Train du Nord, the Little Train of the North, was a laughing stock during its lifetime, a branch line which never made a profit in any of its 100 years of operation. French-Canadian singer-songwriter Félix Leclerc even wrote a song about its pitifully empty carriages. In rough translation:

> Oh, on the train to Sainte-Adèle
> There is only one passenger,
> And that man is the guard.
> What a sad way to travel,
> It would break a heart most hard.

In the mid-twentieth century the line served such tourism as there was for summer hiking and winter skiing in the mountains. The route is therefore well provided with accommodation, refreshments and supplies along its length, although settlements are fewer and further between in the last stages.

The tracks were finally pulled up in the 1990s, although one section of the original track survives in the section from Montreal to Saint-Jérôme. This was the first section of the track to be built, on the orders of the Catholic priest in charge of the settlement of the Laurentians in the nineteenth century. He is remembered as 'the apostle of colonization', and you can see a larger-than-life statue of Father Labelle in the town.

Saint-Jérôme is regarded as the gateway to the Laurentian Mountains; it is from here that this

OPPOSITE: The ski resort of Mont-Tremblant in autumn.

BELOW: Lac Gauvin, Belleterre, Quebec.

BOTTOM LEFT AND RIGHT: Minimum grade changes make the trail perfect for cross-country skiing in winter.

169

trail begins or ends. You can leave your car here and take a shuttle service to Mont-Laurier at the northern end from which most cyclists start.

Mont-Laurier is a centre of the logging industry, originally founded to supply timber and fuel to Montreal – the main reason the P'tit Train was constructed. It sits on rapids of the Du Lièvre river, which were harnessed to provide power to the sawmills. Heading south-east from here the trail skirts the southern shores of Lac des Écorces and Lac Gauvin outside the town. As a former railway the gradients are easy, climbing gently through forests to the township and lake of Lac-Saguay. From there it's a downhill run to Nominique, the first major settlement on the route, 60 km out from Mont-Laurier.

Watch out for shelters along the route in the style of old railway cars. The old station houses have found new uses too. In Nominique the station house has become a tourist information centre; and in Labelle further along the track it is now a restaurant, opposite which an old caboose has been converted into a museum about the trail's railway days. At Labelle the trail changes from a paved surface to one of packed crushed stone. Be aware that on both surfaces the sheer number of cyclists is taking its toll on the road condition.

Beyond Labelle, named after Saint-Jérôme's favourite priest, is Mont-Tremblant, the halfway point on the trail. This is a lively town, and nearby is the livelier Mont-Tremblant Resort Village, an artificial Alpine Town built to accommodate visitors to the nearby ski slopes but open all year. Mont-Tremblant is a literal translation of the old Algonquin name for the place, 'trembling mountain'. It sits alongside Devil's River, and also boasts a golf course and a motor-racing track.

After Mont-Tremblant, at Saint-Jovite, there is a slight but long ascent to the highest point on the trail. Thereafter it's downhill all the way. Sainte-Agathe-des-Monts, the next large settlement,

is the nearest thing to a city in the Laurentians. Founded in 1849, it originally attracted poor Catholics because the landowner was too kind-hearted to ask for rent. Property prices soon soared when it became popular with the sick and the wealthy – the former coming for the healing properties of the mountain air and the latter staying to build their country houses far from Montreal and the northern US.

Just outside Sainte-Agathe, the Rivière du Nord flows out of Lac Brûlé. This is the river that gave the railway its name, and from here on, the trail follows the Val du Nord for the final 50 km or so, all the way to Saint-Jérôme. It passes through Val-David, beloved of writers, artists and musicians, where there is a series of waterfalls and the Parc des Amoureux – the Lovers' Park.

BELOW: A tour boat on the Lac des Sables passes Sainte-Agathe-des-Monts.

BOTTOM: The Rivière du Nord/North River tumbles along near Val-David.

At Sainte-Adèle, of which Félix Leclerc sang, the station is divided between a good restaurant and a splendid bicycle shop. It makes the perfect final rest stop before the trail enters its closing stages on urban bike paths in Saint-Jérôme. If you started cycling from this end, the shuttle bus will bring you back here from Mont-Laurier. Although strictly speaking the trail continues on paths into the Quebecois suburb of Blainville, most people still consider Saint-Jérôme to be Kilometre Zero.

Most families spend three or four days on the trail, making time for picnics, walks and river dips along the way. If you're fit and not interested in scenery, you could certainly complete it in a day – but why ride Le P'tit Train du Nord if you're not interested in the scenery?

RIGHT: Saint-Jérôme Cathedral.

BELOW: The old rail track follows the course of the Rivière du Nord. Hence the name.

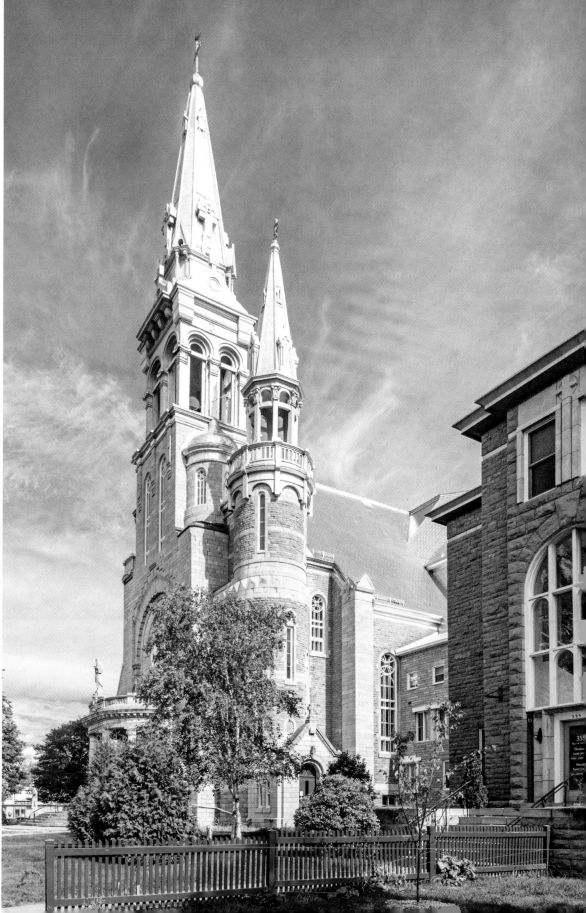

The Parenzana

Italy, Slovenia, Croatia

Length: 123 km, 76 miles
Start: Trieste
Finish: Poreč
Highlights: Trieste Railway Museum and coffee houses, Piran waterfront and salt pans, old locomotives at Grožnjan and Vižinada, Baredine Cave, Poreč Marafor Square

Mussolini closed the little railway line between the Italian cities of Trieste and Parenzo in 1935. Seventy years later a joint project reopened the route to walkers and cyclists and named it the Route of Health and Friendship.

In 1902 a new narrow-gauge railway was built between fashionable, stylish Trieste and the tourist resort of Parenzo in the ancient region of Istria. Trieste was then the fourth-largest city in the Austro-Hungarian Empire, Parenzo, on the Dalmatian coast, an important ship-building centre for the otherwise landlocked empire. The Parenzo line, the Parenzaner Bahn, was an economic success and flourished even after the region was ceded to Italy in 1918 following the dismantling of the Austro-Hungarian Empire.

Now called the Parenzana, its fortunes took a downturn during the global recession of the 1920s and 1930s, and in 1935 Mussolini ordered the closure of the line. After World War II, Parenzo was occupied by Croatian partisans and became part of Yugoslavia. In 1947 it was renamed Poreč.

Following the break-up of Yugoslavia in 1991, the old route of the Parenzana now found itself passing through three separate countries: Italy, Slovenia and Croatia. The development of the route as a cross-border cooperative project was seen as a way to heal some of the divisions of the twentieth century's many conflicts. In 2006 work began on making the old trackbed accessible to cyclists and walkers, and the full Route of Health and Friendship is now open, using some 94% of the original railway line.

Trieste remains a cultural outpost of Mitteleuropa, located on the Adriatic. Its architecture and coffee houses are more Viennese than Venetian, and well worth spending some time in before you set off. If you're interested in the route's railway history, visit the Railway Museum in the city.

The original line had 35 stations, many of which survive and have been put to different uses. A lot of the line's engineering infrastructure is also still in place. The Parenzana passes through eight tunnels and crosses seven viaducts, and its gentle gradient climbs to only 293 metres (961 ft) above sea level. Mountain bikes are recommended because of the occasional rough surface of the track.

The Parenzana is comfortably achievable in two or three days and there is plenty of accommodation along the way. Piran is a medieval gem on the Slovenian coast, with age-old salt pans. As you approach Poreč, look out for the Baredine Cave, a natural formation containing stalactites and stalagmites, which is open to the public. Poreč itself retains the ground plan of the Roman camp over which it was built, and two Roman temples survive on Marafor Square. The town's Euphrasian Basilica is an internationally important sixth-century Christian church.

The development of the Parenzana has played an important part in reuniting the divided communities of Istria and opening them up to the rest of the world again. Health and Friendship are, after all, why cyclists cycle.

OPPOSITE: Trieste's Canal Grande, Italy.

ABOVE RIGHT: The waterfront at Piran, Slovenia.

RIGHT: One of eight tunnels on the route, this one in Slovenia.

Paris to Mont St Michel

France

Length: 450 km, 280 miles
Start: Paris
Finish: Mont St Michel
Highlights: Palace of Versailles, Château de la Madeleine, Rambouillet palaces and Rambolitrain Museum, Maintenon, Chartres Cathedral, Maison Picassiette, Château de Carrouges, Bagnoles-de-l'Orne, Pontaubault Bridge, Mont St Michel

The centuries-old journey from Paris to Mont St Michel has been made by pilgrims and prisoners, soldiers and sightseers, kings and clergymen. For cyclists, the route on traffic-free *voies vertes* and back roads is a meditation on the history of France.

The countryside west of Paris is some of the most beautiful in France, and the cycle route through it is known as the Veloscenic. It passes through several regional nature parks as well as a succession of historic town centres.

There are several routes south-west out of Paris, all of them quite urban, and many cyclists choose to start their Veloscenic in the more glamorous surroundings of the Palace of Versailles on the edge of the city. From that man-made splendour the trail leads through the Chevreuse Regional Nature Park, a rural area surrounding the valley of the Yvette river. It's studded with Baroque palaces, grand country houses and the rock-top fortified Château de la Madeleine.

The Forest of Rambouillet lies on the south-western edge of the Chevreuse; and in

Rambouillet itself stand not one but two royal palaces, reminders of a time when hunting in the forest was the preserve of kings. The town is also home to the Rambolitrain Museum of miniature railways.

The route continues to Chartres by way of Maintenon, where Louis XIV, the Sun King, kept his second wife in a charming palace in the centre of the town. She was a woman of 'low' birth who could never be admitted to court in Paris. From Maintenon Louis had an aqueduct constructed purely for the purpose of watering the gardens of Versailles, some 55 km to the north-east.

Chartres Cathedral is one of the architectural glories of the world, little changed or damaged since its construction in the thirteenth century. The city has many other medieval charms and, at the other end of the architectural scale, the Maison Picassiette. This house was built and decorated inside and out with fragments of pottery by one man, Raymond Isadore, from the 1930s to the 1960s.

Literary-minded cyclists will recognize the name of the town of Illiers-Combray beyond Chartres. Illiers adopted its other half after Marcel Proust modelled the fictional town of Combray on it in his seven-volume semi-autobiographical novel *A la Recherche du Temps Perdu* ('In search of Lost Time'). West of Illiers the Veloscenic enters the Perche Nature Park, a huge area of agriculture and native forest which has been inhabited since

TOP: The exquisite Palace of Versailles.

ABOVE: Champ des Epins forest road in the Forest of Rambouillet.

OPPOSITE: Heading into the department of Eure-et-Loir, the aqueduct and château at Maintenon.

the Stone Age. It is said that almost every French Canadian can trace their ancestors to the villages of the Perche. In the thirteenth century the region was controlled by two families, and the fortress of one of them, the Château Saint-Jean, still stands in Nogent-le-Rotrou, a lengthy climb and descent beyond Chartres. (The other was in Bellême, to the south of the Veloscenic route but worth a detour for its seventeenth-century town centre.)

After ascending the high plateau on the western edge of the Perche the route descends to Alençon in Normandy, famous for lace-making and printing. The dukes of Alençon built themselves a forbidding fortress here. Alençon is surrounded on three sides by the extensive Normandie-Maine Natural Park, an area of pretty villages nestled in the forests and protected by castles and noble country homes. Fortification and comfort are combined in the Château de Carrouges, to which the Veloscenic climbs at gentle length from Alençon. As a fourteenth-century moated castle it was destroyed by the English during the Hundred Years' War, and rebuilt over the next 300 years with increasingly grand living apartments.

The trail descends in stages to Bagnoles-de-l'Orne, a spa town since the Middle Ages which reached its zenith in the early twentieth century.

It boasts some exquisite Belle Époque and Art Deco architecture. The 1927 lakeside casino attracted such wealthy clients as the King and Queen of Romania and Princes and Princesses of Greece, Montenegro and Battenberg.

By contrast the heydays of Domfront, west of Bagnoles, were in medieval times. Its narrow streets grew up around the eleventh-century castle, which now lies in ruins in the town park. It was here in 1128 that Henry II of England met delegates from the Pope who hoped to bring about his reconciliation with his 'meddlesome priest', Archbishop Thomas Becket of Canterbury. The town itself, fortified separately, retains many towers, half-timbered buildings and grand old townhouses.

Now the Veloscenic descends gently to the wide flat plain of the Sélune river as it makes its way to the sea. Pause to admire the Pontaubault Bridge over the river, a beautiful stone-arched structure built in the fifteenth century and still in use today. It even survived General Patton's VIII Corps,

TOP LEFT: Chartres and its epic flying buttressed cathedral.

TOP: The river Sarthe and the Notre Dame Basilica at Alençon in Normandy.

ABOVE: Bar Normand in Domfront is typical of the half-timbered 'colombage' buildings throughout Normandy.

which crossed it – the only surviving bridge in the area in August 1944 – on their way to liberate Paris. Mont St Michel is just around the corner.

Pilgrims travelling to the holy site of Mont St Michel nicknamed it 'St Michael's in Peril from the Sea' because of the dangerous tides surrounding it. Today a new bridge replaces the old causeway. It was opened in 2014 and consists of a pedestrian walkway and a bus lane. No other traffic is allowed, and that includes bikes. There are three designated bicycle parks. The crossing is a 35-minute walk, or a free shuttle bus.

The Veloscenic is a relaxed, easy-going trail, well signposted and away from busy roads. Accommodation is plentiful and access is easy by train at either end. At Domfront the route crosses the Vélo Francette, a route from northern Normandy to La Rochelle on the Atlantic coast. Mont St Michel also sits on EuroVelo 4.

RIGHT AND BELOW: Two views of Mont St Michel. In the past, visitors could drive all the way up to the UNESCO World Heritage Site. Now they have to walk or take a bus along the causeway. Cyclists are permitted between October and April.

Cycling on the Postal Boat

Norway

Length: Around 50 km, 31 miles

Highlights: Utvær Lighthouse, Hardbakke Arboretum, Gåsvær, Bulandet, Geita Lighthouse, Værøyhamna Harbour

Norway isn't necessarily the first place you think of for cycling – all those deep, steep, long fjords. But the country is fringed with a scattering of islands interconnected by causeways and bridges which are perfect for a few days' exploration by bicycle.

The island communities of Solund, Bulandet and Værlandet are a popular destination. They are Norway's most westerly islands and lie just north of Bergen. Ferries from the mainland to Solund leave from Rutledal and Rysjedalsvika Ferjekai, either side of Sognefjord, the longest (205 km) and deepest (1,308 metres/4,291 ft) in Norway. Værlandet ferries depart from Askvoll and Fure on Dalsfjord.

Transport between the islands is with the local mail boat which sails from Hardbakke on Solund's largest island, Sula. During the summer months there is a commentary for visitors about local history and wildlife. For cyclists the attraction is the web of roads between all of these – sometimes tiny – patches of land, some inhabited by just one household. Solund alone consists of over 1,700 islands.

It is possible to do a round trip of all three island groups in a day with an express boat from Bergen. It takes a little over twelve hours and leaves you less than three hours in total for any cycling. Better by far to base yourself on one of the islands and spend a few days exploring, as opposed to staring at ferry timetables.

There's plenty on offer. On the exposed islands of Solund, it's no surprise to find a lighthouse. Its keepers are the only residents now of the most westerly island of all, Utvær. Utvær once had a wooden chapel big enough for a congregation of 120. In the seventeenth century it was pillaged by pirates from Scotland – presumably descendants of the Vikings who pillaged Scotland in the first millennium.

Between Solund and Bulandet is the remote island group of Gåsvær. The last permanent residents left in 1990, and now all the houses are holiday homes. But, situated near Norway's vital fishing grounds, Gåsvær has a long history of self-sufficiency and trade in an often hostile environment.

Nowadays Bulandet is the most westerly active fishing port in Norway. The name comes from the 'bu', or cabins, which line the wharf. It's the main village in the Bulandet archipelago, and during World War II it acted as a vital departure point for the so-called Shetland Bus, a covert operation run by the Norwegian Navy in exile in the Shetland archipelago north of mainland Scotland. South of Bulandet, you can rent Geita Lighthouse in the summer. In the winter it is run as an artists' retreat.

Bulandet and Værlandet archipelagos sit side by side, now connected from east to west by 5 km of roads and six bridges. Besides fishing, Værlandet exports a high-grade breccia decorative stone to Italy. Værøyhamna Harbour in the north-east of Værlandet is lined with picturesque houses.

Wildlife is abundant in these islands. White-tailed eagles are a common sight, and the inshore waters are populated with seals and otters. The cycling is easy here. But bring protection against the weather, an occupational hazard of island life.

OPPOSITE: The lighthouse at Utvær, the most westerly inhabited island in Norway.

BELOW: Houses at Gåsvær on Kvalfjord, near Troms.

BOTTOM: Many islands have been linked by an ingenious pattern of bridges.

Route of the Hiawatha

Montana and Idaho, USA

Length: 15 miles, 24 km
Start: Lookout Pass, Montana
Finish: Pearson, Idaho
Highlights: St Paul Pass Tunnel, Kelly Creek Trestle, Adair Loop, Clear Creek Trestle

The forbidding terrain of the Bitterroot Mountains between Montana and Idaho was a tough nut for the Chicago, Milwaukee and Puget Sound Railroads to crack. Since the line's closure in 1980 it has become one of the most scenic short bike trails in America.

The route took three years to survey and another two to construct, involving the digging of ten tunnels and the building of seven high trestle bridges. Costs ballooned from an original estimate in 1906 of $43 million to an eye-watering $234 million by the time it was completed.

The line rarely made a profit in its early years, but after World War II it was the route of two glamorous trains, the Hiawatha to the Midwest, and the Olympian Hiawatha from Chicago to Seattle. Nevertheless, the expansion of car ownership and the availability of internal flights hit hard, and by 1961 the last passenger train had run over the rails.

The cyclists' Route of the Hiawatha is only a short part of the thousands of miles of the original Milwaukee Railroad. In Washington State it has become the John Wayne Pioneer Trail, and in Idaho and Montana more and more of the route is being developed for cycling. Today the Hiawatha is described as the Crown Jewel of America's many rail-to-trail bike routes. It starts seven miles from the Lookout Pass skiing area near Wallace, and bikes can be rented here. A permit is required to ride the trail, which you can

buy at the trailhead, East Portal, where there are rest rooms and a car park.

The trailhead gets its name from the trail's first major feature, the East Portal to the St Paul Pass Tunnel, the longest on the route at 1.66 miles. Even when it's dry and sunny outside it can be cold and muddy in there, so bring warm clothing. Above you as you cycle through it is the border between Montana and Idaho and the snaking St Paul Pass. The trail emerges at Roland above Cliff Creek and follows it south downstream for a while before turning sharply east.

The stretch of the trail from Roland is a shared road, but as it crosses Moss Creek cyclists once again have it all to themselves, following Loop Creek upstream. As the valley climbs, the trackbed descends, tunnelling through ridges and flying over valleys on towering trestles. One minute you are above the treetops; the next you are under their roots.

The drop through the St Paul Pass Tunnel is only 27 ft (8 metres), but by the time the road makes a dramatic 180-degree turn at Adair – the Loop which gave the creek its name – it has descended another 400 ft (122 metres). As you follow Loop Creek back downstream to the end of the trail at Pearson, it will descend nearly 600 ft (183 metres) more. This trail is all downhill, and if you don't want to cycle back up to the car park, coaches from Pearson will ferry you and your bike there via the St Paul Pass.

ABOVE RIGHT: It's an exhilarating experience cycling at speed through the tree tops.

RIGHT: The entrance to the Taft Tunnel.

OPPOSITE: 'Riding the trestles' on the Hiawatha in Idaho.

Route des Grands Crus

France

Length: 60 km, 37 miles
Start: Dijon
Finish: Santenay
Highlights: Chenôve, Château du Clos de Vougeot, Hôtel-Dieu de Beaune, the two Châteaux de Pommard, Château de Santenay

Here's a bike ride for cyclists of stern discipline. It's not the route which will challenge you but the temptations along the way - the cellars of some of the oldest and noblest wines in France.

Wines have been produced on the slopes of Burgundy for around 2,000 years, and practice makes perfect. The region is best known for its dry reds, made from the Pinot noir grape, and also produces fine whites from Chardonnay vines.

The most highly prized (and priced) of them come from a tiny area on the eastern slopes of the Vosges Mountains, less than 50 km long and often as little as 2 km in width. What makes these vineyards so special? Perhaps there's something in the water; after all, several world-famous brands of mineral water are drawn from Vosges springs. Whatever the reason, this short stretch of hallowed ground is known as the Côte d'Or, the Golden Hillside. The best wines from here are called Grands Crus.

On the Route des Grands Crus you will have ample opportunity to taste them for yourself in the cellars of the great and the good of Burgundy. Starting from Dijon the route passes through nearly 40 charming villages, each with their own historic connection to the wine. From Chenôve to Corgoloin you are in the Côte de Nuits, the northern half of the Côte d'Or. Within these few kilometres lie no fewer than 24 of

Burgundy's Grands Crus, including Chambertin, Clos de Vougeot, Romanée-Conti and Nuits-Saint-Georges.

At Chenôve you can see the wine presses of Philip the Bold, the fourteenth-century Duke of Burgundy. The Clos, at Vougeot and elsewhere, are enclosed vineyards, surrounded by limestone walls and often with a grand stone archway for an entrance. Many of the clos are associated with châteaux, a grand counterpoint to the simplicity of the villages from which each vineyard's workers were recruited.

Beyond Corgoloin the Côte de Nuits gives way to the Côte de Beaune, where some of the world's best dry white wines, the Chardonnays, are made – among them Corton-Charlemagne and vintages from the villages of Meursault and Montrachet. They are centred on the town of Beaune, with its stunning fifteenth-century almshouses and the Hôtel-Dieu, 'God's hostel'.

The route ends at another of Philip the Bold's castles, the fourteenth-century Château de Santenay. Here you can sample burgundies of a more rustic nature than the Grands Crus further north.

With a height variation of less than 100 metres (328 ft) throughout its short length, this is on paper an easy ride. But plan ahead - you will have to strike a balance between tasting and touring. Bring empty panniers and something to cushion all the bottles you won't be able to resist buying along the way.

TOP: Hôtel-Dieu de Beaune.

MIDDLE: Les Gravières vineyard in Santenay.

BOTTOM: One of France's most exclusive wine-growing *terroirs*.

OPPOSITE: Château du Clos de Vougeot, Cote d'Or, Burgundy.

Salzach Valley

Austria

Length: 310 km, 193 miles

Start: Krimml

Finish: Passau

Highlights: Krimml Waterfalls, Pinzgauer Lokalbahn, Kaprun Lake, Liechtensteinklamm, Eisriesenwelt, Golling Waterfall, Hallein Salt Mine, Salzburg, Burghausen Castle, Adolf Hitler's Birthplace

From its source in the Tyrolean Alps to its confluence with the Danube, the Salzach river in western Austria sweeps you past waterfalls, caves, salt mines and lakes, and through beautiful Austrian villages and towns.

You could easily spend a week of leisurely sightseeing and cycling on this well-supported route. It's comprehensively signposted, first as the Tauernradweg ('Tauern Bicycle Trail'), and after the Salzach joins the river Inn as the Innradweg. There is plenty of accommodation along the way, and unrivalled alpine scenery to lift your heart as well as your pedalling feet. Mozart and *The Sound of Music* make an appearance too.

The route starts in Krimml, a small town serving the nearby Oberkrimml skiing area, where the Salzach river has its source. Here the Krimml

brook, one of the highest sequences of waterfalls in Europe, thunders down from the mountains to join the Salzach 380 metres (1,247 ft) below. Your own journey will be much gentler: this trail descends through forests and meadows, small villages and towns, mostly on dedicated cycle paths or quiet roads. It's almost all downhill with only a few short sharp climbs.

From Krimml the Salzach flows north-east between the Kitzbühel Alps to the north and the High Tauern mountain range to the south. In the first few kilometres you pass below the Grossglockner, the highest peak in Austria (3,798 metres/12,461 ft). The economy here relies on dairy farming and winter sports. So for example at Bramberg, in season, there is a 14-km-long floodlit toboggan run; and in Hollersbach a little further downstream there's a festival every September to celebrate bringing

OPPOSITE: The lower Krimml waterfall.

TOP: High above Kaprun is the Mooserboden Reservoir.

MIDDLE: Take a detour and get some great views of the lake at Zell am See.

RIGHT: The Grossglockner High Alpine Road near the Emperor Franz Joseph monument.

the cows in from the high pastures in preparation for winter. Kaprun, watched over by its twelfth-century castle, is typical of many villages – in the winter it's a small skiing resort with cable cars to the north-facing slopes; and in the summer a short detour will take you up to the sky-blue glacial meltwaters of Kaprun Lake. For those who followed the HBO series *Band of Brothers* – it's

also where Easy Company ended up after World War II hostilities ceased.

The town of Bruck is an important crossroads. *Bruck* means 'bridge', and besides being a crossing point over the Salzach, the road north leads to another well-travelled cycling route, the Saalachtal. The road to the south is the famous

ABOVE: Panorama of Hohenwerfen Castle and Berchtesgaden Alps, location of Hitler's Eagle's Nest retreat.

OPPOSITE TOP: View from Mönchsberg Hill looking across the Salzach river and Salzburg.

OPPOSITE BOTTOM: The Residenzbrunnen Fountain in the centre of Salzburg *does* appear in *The Sound of Music*, but viewed from the left of this photo.

Grossglockner High Alpine Road, the highest paved road in Europe. It was built in 1935 purely to be a scenic drive for the new car-owning classes, and its hairpin twists and turns are as popular with cyclists as with motorists. There is a toll for its use, and it is closed in the winter months when snow pervades.

Naturally the valley floor, with its easy gradient, is attractive not only to cyclists but in the past to railway builders, and you have the company of rail tracks for most of its length. Krimml is served by a narrow-gauge train, the Pinzgauer Lokalbahn, until Zell am See just north of Bruck, where it connects with a mainline route, the Salzburg-Tyrol line, or Giselabahn. The route of the Giselabahn west of Bruck, through Zell and Kitzbühel to Wörgl, is one of the world's great scenic railway routes.

Beyond Schwarzach the valley turns northwards on its way to Salzburg. A couple of detours are worth making. Near Grafenhof there's a spectacular gorge, the Liechtensteinklamm, 300 metres (984 ft) deep and in places only a few metres wide, with a walkway along its base. Before Tenneck, Hohenwerfen Castle occupies a commanding position above a bend in the river. Above the village you can visit Ice Giant World, Eisriesenwelt, a 42-km network of limestone caves of which the first kilometre, open to the public, is lined in ice all year round. The cave system was formed millennia ago by the Salzach river. Near the town of Golling it's a short walk to the high-spilling Golling Waterfall.

One of the highlights of the route is a visit to the Salt Mine at Hallein. The earliest working of the mine was at least 7,000 years ago, and the precious resource of salt, 'salz' in German, gave the river and its principle town Salzburg their names. A 90-minute guided tour includes an electric train ride, descents on a wooden slide, and a boat trip across an underground lake.

Salzburg, Austria's fourth largest city, is a Baroque gem and the birthplace of Wolfgang Amadeus Mozart, something you are never allowed to forget while you're there. It also supplied many of the locations for the film *The Sound of Music*. Fans of the movie can join in a sing-along bike tour of Salzburg with Fräulein Maria. The Mirabell Gardens meeting point is a very good place to start.

Salzburg is dominated by one of the largest medieval castles in Europe, the Hohensalzburg Fortress. Here the Salzach is joined by the Saalach, and cyclists have the option of making this a circular trail by following the Saalach upstream as it winds in and out of Austria and Germany. You rejoin the Salzach river near Bruck for the ride back to Krimml. For those with weary legs the Pinzgauer Lokalbahn to Krimml starts in Zell.

North of Salzburg, the villages of Oberndorf and Laufen, on opposite sides of a bridge over the Salzach, were one town until the German-Austrian border was redrawn in 1816 after the Napoleonic Wars; Oberndorf lies on the Austrian side. Now the river forms the border for the rest of the trail. On Christmas Eve 1818, Oberndorf's priest and schoolmaster premiered their new hymn 'Silent Night' in the village, and a memorial chapel commemorates the eternally popular Christmas carol.

At Duttendorf you will see, on the skyline across the water in Germany, Burghausen Castle, the longest castle in the world. Just beyond the village of Überackern we say goodbye to the Salzach as its waters merge with the Inn. The Inn

TOP LEFT: A memorial chapel in Oberndorf dedicated to the composers of 'Silent Night'.

TOP RIGHT: The Salzachbrücke from Oberndorf to Laufen.

LEFT: Aerial view of Burghausen Castle on the Inn River. It is the world's longest castle.

rises near St Moritz in Switzerland before making its 518-km journey through Austria, via Innsbruck, then Germany. From Überackern downstream it marks the border between the two countries.

The first major town through which it now passes is Braunau am Inn and its Bavarian counterpart Simbach am Inn on the German side. Braunau is a pretty town overshadowed by its notoriety as the birthplace of Adolf Hitler. The house in which he was born still stands and currently serves as a 'House of Responsibility', documenting the man's crimes against humanity. Braunau was also the birthplace of its former mayor Hans Staininger, who in 1567 died after he broke his neck by tripping over his own 1.4-metre-long beard, having forgotten to roll it up as usual in a specially made leather pouch.

The Inn does not have much further to go now. The way is punctuated by a string of pretty riverside villages until at last it comes to a full stop in Passau, just across the river in Germany. Here the Inn joins forces with the Danube. Passau has a charming medieval centre and is the starting point for cruises and bike trails up and down the Danube.

This is an easy cycle route, with plenty to see and do for the family along the way. Its connection to other trails in the area – along the Danube, up the Saalachtal and over the Grossglocknerstrasse – means it can be woven into a much longer cycling holiday for the serious rider. And you won't have to climb every mountain or ford any streams.

RIGHT: The confluence of three rivers in Passau: the Danube, Inn and Ilz.

San Juan Islands

Washington State, USA

Length: Up to 400 miles, 644 km
Start/Finish: Anacortes WA
Highlights: Deception Pass Bridge, Mount Constitution, Little Red Schoolhouse, Lime Kiln Point, British and American camps, Odlin Park, Shark Reef Park

The San Juan Islands are a diamond-shaped, low-lying archipelago off the north-west coast of Washington State. Reached only by ferries, they are a haven of quiet roads and rich wildlife, and a mecca for photographers and cyclists.

The waters just south of the 49th parallel were explored more or less simultaneously by Britain and Spain, although as you can tell from their name, Spain found the San Juan Islands first. Occupying the waters at the border of Canada and the US, they have often been the subject of territorial dispute. In 1859 the US and the UK even came to blows over the islands in the so-called Pig War (the conflict escalated after the shooting of a pig).

Because of their joint discovery and various changes of ownership, many coastal features in the area have had different names over the centuries; it was only in 2010 that Canada and the US finally agreed on a name for the waters which surround the San Juan Islands – the Salish Sea (the Salish people were the aboriginal inhabitants).

Of the more than 100 islands and rocky outcrops which make up the archipelago, four are served

OPPOSITE: Connecting Whidbey Island to Fidalgo Island, the epic Deception Pass Bridge.

BELOW LEFT: Moran State Park on Orcas Island.

BELOW: There's a rich variety of waterfalls and fallen trees in Moran State Park.

by vehicle and passenger ferries operated by the state of Washington. Any one of the four makes a good day's cycling, and the weather is reliably warm and sunny, with lower rainfall than average for the area. The whole group adds up to a relaxing week's cycling holiday.

The city of Anacortes is the starting-off point for the islands. Anacortes was founded with the intention of becoming the western terminus of the Northern Pacific Railroad. The tracks never reached it and the city flourished instead as a fishing port and timber milling centre. Anacortes is on Fidalgo Island, not technically part of the San Juan group but separated from the mainland by the narrow Swinomish Channel. Fidalgo offers a 24-mile circuit of roads for cyclists, which can be extended by crossing the striking Deception Pass Bridge onto Whidbey Island. Deception Pass is a narrow sea channel with dramatic currents when the tide is running at its fastest. The rugged, wooded land on either side of it forms Deception Pass State Park.

RIGHT: Friday Harbor on San Juan Island.

BELOW: Lime Kiln Lighthouse on the west coast of San Juan Island.

There are no bridges between any of the San Juan Islands. Ferries from Anacortes serve several of them as well as the Canadian port of Sidney on Vancouver Island. Orcas Island makes a good starting point and a base from which to explore the others. It's a double-horseshoe shape, curled around the sheltered waters of West and East Sound. The village of Eastsound at its head is the island's largest settlement.

Orcas, with acres of forestry, is known as the Emerald Isle. There are miles of quiet byways to explore, and on windless days the reflection of the trees in the island's lakes and harbours is balm for the soul. Most of Orcas is less than 500 ft (152 metres) above sea level, but it also boasts the highest peak (by far) in the islands, Mount Constitution, at 2,116 ft (645 metres). You can ride the steep road through the trees to the lookout tower at the top, from which the view over the whole archipelago is not to be missed. The unusual shape and contours of Orcas Island means that a coastal circuit of the island is not possible. To ride to all its corners and highpoints might involve a round trip of 50–70 miles; it's well worth making your visit to Orcas a two-day stay.

It's a short ride from the south coast of Orcas to Shaw Island, the smallest of the San Juans to be

served by ferry. There are less than a dozen miles of paved roads here, and tourist businesses are banned from Shaw to preserve its rural character. It has a permanent population of 240, a general store open only in the summer months and a museum of the island's interesting history. The Little Red Schoolhouse, built in 1891, is the oldest working school in Washington, and Shaw Island's quiet way of life has proved attractive to several religious institutions over the years. Until 2004, Franciscan nuns ran the store and the ferry terminal.

West of Shaw Island is the largest landmass in the group, San Juan Island. The first permanent non-native settlement here was by the Hudson Bay Company in 1853, and it was the death of a Company piglet at the hands of an American settler that sparked the Pig War in 1859. Although no shots were fired and no human lives lost in the 'war', the absurd dispute rumbled

TOP LEFT: English Camp at Garrison Bay.

TOP RIGHT: Roche Harbor filled to near capacity. The islands are a boater's paradise.

ABOVE: Looking more like the Midwest, this is Cattle Point Road on San Juan Island.

on until 1872. The remains of the opposing British and American camps are preserved at either end of the island.

Today the island is a popular escape from city life. Friday Harbor, where the ferry arrives, is the main settlement on the island. If you want a break from cycling, whale-watching cruises depart from here. Although Orcas Island got its name from the Mexican Viceroy (Horcasitas) who sent an expedition in 1791, the San Juan Islands do have a number of resident orca pods. Even if you do not take a cruise, you may see one from your bike on one of the coastal roads. There is also a Whale Museum in Friday Harbor.

The highest point on the island is Mount Dallas, though at 1,080 ft (329 metres) it's hardly worthy of the name and there are few roads more than 350 ft above sea level. As you'd expect with coastal roads, there are plenty of short climbs and descents to get around promontories and cliffs, but the cycling is easy here. Don't miss Lime Kiln Point Lighthouse on the west coast or tree-lined Roche Harbor in the north. A typical circuit of San Juan Island is about 45 miles, further if you explore inland too.

The longest beaches on the island are South Beach and Fourth of July Beach – they are a mixture of sand and pebbles, often strewn with timber storm debris, and are consequently great places for wildlife. Besides orcas, the islands are home to minke whales and Dall's porpoise, Steller sea lions and river otters; and beavers, which the Hudson Bay Company hunted to extinction here, have recently begun to return. There is a rich variety of tree species on the islands, and a correspondingly rich bird population: great blue herons and trumpeter swans; diving seabirds like the rhinoceros auklet and the rare marbled murrelet; and several birds of prey including harriers, falcons and owls all thrive here. The islands also have the largest population of bald eagles in the contiguous 48 states.

Between San Juan Island and Fidalgo Island lies Lopez Island, the most low-lying of the major islands of the archipelago and the most popular with cyclists. The roads are quieter too, and there is a long-standing tradition on Lopez

BELOW: Sunset falls on Fisherman's Bay, Lopez Island.

of waving at all who pass, be they pedestrians, cyclists or motorists. The island is blessed with several coastal parks: Odlin Park near the ferry terminal in the north of the island has one of the best sandy beaches in the San Juan Islands, while Otis Perkins Park has one of the longest. Shark Reef Park in the south contains some of the oldest woodlands of the islands along its rocky shoreline. Iceberg Point in the far south-west of the island gives uninterrupted views of the mountainous Olympic Peninsula to the south and Vancouver Island to the west. A full circuit of Lopez Island is about 45 miles long.

The San Juan Islands make an exciting destination for a family cycling holiday. The rides are not too demanding and the rewards of scenery and island life are infinite. Bring your camera and a bird-spotting guide.

ABOVE: Almost there – the ferry to Anacortes can get busy in peak season.

LEFT: Shark Reef sanctuary on Lopez Island.

Shimanami Kaido Bikeway

Japan

Length: 76 km, 47 miles
Start: Onomichi
Finish: Imabari
Highlights: Innoshima Suigun Castle, Kosanji Temple, Tatara Bridge, Oyamazumi Shrine, Kurushima-Kaikyo Bridge, the off-ramp at Imabari

One of Japan's most popular cycle trails offers terrific views of Japan, both ancient and modern. It links main island Honshu with nearby Shikoku using six other islands as stepping stones, all with dedicated cycle lanes and traffic-free paths.

The Shimanami Kaido Bikeway crosses the Seto Inland Sea on seven magnificent bridges, including the longest series of suspension bridges in the world and the world's longest cable-stayed bridge. If you're indifferent to bridges you'll just have to make do with acres of citrus groves, ancient temples, pirate lairs and shimmering views of the Seto Sea National Park.

The bridges were built to carry the Nishiseto Expressway, a four-lane highway connecting two of Japan's five main islands. The Bikeway shares the bridges in safely separate bike lanes, but otherwise uses quiet roads and paths on the six small islands over which the highway passes.

The only gradients are the on- and off-ramps at either end of the bridges. The first of these, in Onomichi, is quite steep, and cyclists can avoid it by catching a ferry for the short crossing to Mukaishima, picking up the trail there. In the south of the island, there's a popular beach resort at Tachibana before Innoshima suspension bridge carries you over to the island of the same name.

Innoshima was a refuge for the pirates who controlled the Seto Sea for three hundred years

from the fourteenth to the sixteenth century. Today their impressive castle houses a museum about their activities. From Innoshima the trail continues to Ikuchijima, Japan's largest producer of citrus fruit. In the major town, Setoda, there are several traditional temples and shrines.

The world's longest cable-stayed bridge, the Tatara Bridge (1,480 metres/4,855 ft) leaves Ikuchijima for Omishima, a largely rural island. There's a good museum of marine history here, and if you are cycling the Bikeway over two days this is a good place to spend the night. Near the cyclists' off-ramp are the Tatara Hot Springs.

An elegant steel arched bridge crosses the narrow stretch of water to Hakatajima. The Seto Sea, in which these islands sit, connects the Sea of Japan to the west with the Pacific Ocean, and tide-watching is a memorable experience. For the brave, cruises are available to witness the force of the currents from closer quarters.

From a viewpoint high on the next island, Oshima, you can get a great view of what is to come, the hypnotic towers of the Kurushima-Kaikyo suspension bridge (4,105 metres/13,468 ft), actually a long, straight line of connected suspension bridges which take you finally to Shikoku island and the city of Imabari at journey's end. Take time halfway along the Kurushima to descend by lift to Umashima on tiny Ma island below, for a close-up view of the tidal rapids.

This is a trail rich in interest and, if you're unfamiliar with Japanese culture, a great introduction to it. For a fully immersive cycling experience, stay at the bicycle-friendly Hotel Cycle in Onomichi, where you can take your beloved bike back to your room at night.

TOP: Our start point, Onomichi.

MIDDLE: Many bridges have cycle and pedestrian lanes below the carriageway.

BOTTOM: Sake barrel offerings are left at the Shinto shrine at Umenomiya-Taisha.

OPPOSITE: Kurushima-Kaikyo Bridge at Imabari.

The South Downs Way

England

Length: 100 miles, 161 km
Start: Winchester
Finish: Eastbourne
Highlights: Winchester Cathedral, Cheesefoot Head, Old Winchester Fort, Butser Hill, Bignor, Amberley, Chanctonbury Ring, Steyning, Devil's Dyke, Lewes, Star Inn at Alfriston, the Long Man, Beachy Head

A quintessential English landscape of rolling hills is the setting for a short but challenging MTB trail on a variety of surfaces. This rural route avoids centres of population in favour of timeless views.

The South Downs Way has been a popular walking route for centuries, with easy access for weekend hikers from London to the north. With the recent resurgence of leisure cycling in England, it has become a favourite of pedalheads too.

It is definitely not a dedicated cycling path. English law allows its use by pedestrians and horse-riders too and in valleys and woodlands churned by hooves it can become very muddy. On exposed heights the chalky bedrock, polished by thousands of feet over hundreds of years, can be extremely slippery when wet. Sharp flint in the

soil can also be a hazard, and ordinary road and hybrid bicycles may not be strong enough.

What seems a gently undulating landscape to the walker is a succession of bracing ascents and descents for the cyclist. If you start the trail from Eastbourne you are immediately confronted with a 25% climb, which is a strong argument for starting it from the Winchester end. From Winchester the prevailing winds are at your back as well.

Winchester is a handsome city whose focal point, its Gothic cathedral, has the longest nave in Europe. It was a large settlement even in the Iron Age, and there have been water mills here, powered by the River Itchen, since the tenth century. One still grinds corn today. From Winchester the route climbs the steep flanks of Deacon Hill (with a D) before settling on a gentle upland path past Cheesefoot Head. This large natural amphitheatre was the perfect place for General Eisenhower to address massed American troops on the eve of D-Day in 1944.

Look out for the remains of Lomer, a village abandoned in the fourteenth century after an outbreak of Bubonic Plague. Beacon Hill

LEFT: A section of the South Downs Way cutting through arable fields that were previously grass downland.

OPPOSITE: Long associated with the novels of Anthony Trollope, who lived in the town, Winchester Cathedral is the longest Gothic cathedral in the world.

(with a B) is one of several hills along the route used to signal impending danger in past times. The Way drops down to cross the River Meon at Exton before climbing back up to Old Winchester Fort, an Iron Age defensive position typical of many which crown the hills along the South Downs Way. Another down-and-up takes you onto Salt Hill and the short final ascent of Butser Hill, the highest point on the trail.

The advantage of all these hills is the recurring opportunity for wonderful views across the countryside. Although this corner of England is relatively densely populated, the route that the South Downs Way follows gives an impression of unspoilt pastoral bliss. This is precisely the landscape which the poet William Blake described as 'England's green and pleasant land' – he was living in the village of Felpham, just south of the Way, when he wrote the poem *Jerusalem* from which the line comes.

There's a thrilling descent from Butser Hill before the path climbs again and levels off above the villages of Harting, Cocking and Graffham. If you're doing the trail over three days, any of them makes a good stop for your first night out. Hardened MTB trail riders will be able to complete the route in two long days. There is plenty of accommodation near the route, although little actually on it.

On the slopes of Bignor Hill beyond Graffham, the South Downs Way meets the Monarchs Way, a walking trail on the dead-straight route of the Roman road Stane Street. In the village of Bignor the remains of a Roman villa can be seen, while the hill itself shows the traces of a Neolithic encampment. The trail descends to Amberley, where The Thatched House hotel is one of the few houses in the village which is *not* thatched. The River Arun here is tidal and the marshes to the north a vital wetland habitat for birds.

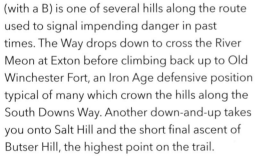

ABOVE LEFT: Chanctonbury Ring Iron Age hill fort near Worthing.

TOP: Heading downhill to the Adur Valley near Upper Beeding and Steyning.

ABOVE: The Barbican Gate at Lewes Castle, East Sussex.

A long, steady climb out of Amberley passes above Storrington: if you're attempting to ride the South Downs Way in two days, you will need to have reached Storrington at the end of the first. A little further on, the Chanctonbury Ring is an impressive hilltop fort with evidence of occupation from the Bronze Age to the Roman era. The descent from here takes you across the River Adur near Steyning and its surrounding villages. These have Anglo-Saxon origins, and Alfred the Great's father, Ethelwulf, was buried here in AD 858.

A couple of long climbs take you up out of the Adur Valley to the Devil's Dyke, a natural V-shaped dry valley used defensively in the Iron Age, when its inhabitants removed all the topsoil to display banks of gleaming white chalk beneath. Legend says the curving valley is the hoofprint of the Devil in goat form. From here the Way continues past Ditchling Beacon, the third highest hill in the South Downs, before descending into Lewes, a busy market town with a medieval castle and many options for accommodation on the second night of a three-day ride.

The final stage from Lewes to Eastbourne starts with a stiff ascent from the River Ouse to Firle Beacon, the last on the South Downs Way of these relay stations from which warning fires would be seen by other beacon hills in the chain. Many prehistoric burial mounds in the area prove that it was a significant place long before recorded history. At the pretty village of Alfriston the ancient Star Inn has connections with pilgrims and smugglers. Here walkers and cyclists part company – walkers head for the coast, while the bike route passes over Windover Hill. From here there is a striking view of the Long Man, the outline of a distinctly masculine figure carved into the chalk in the sixteenth century. After Jevington there's one final punishing ascent to the top of Beachy Head, Britain's highest chalk cliffs, before that

last 25% descent into Eastbourne, the end of the South Downs Way.

Considering the genteel surroundings, this is quite a tough trail. But where there's an ascent, a descent is sure to follow; and a ride through the South Downs is a journey back through thousands of years of England's early history. Unspoilt by modern life, the long views from its hills are glimpses of the past.

ABOVE: Looking back at Lewes and the River Ouse.

RIGHT: To the lighthouse … and past it. The Beachy Head Lighthouse signals that you're very close to your destination in Eastbourne.

Stelvio Pass

Italy

Length: 46 km, 29 miles
Start: Prato/Prad
Finish: Bormio
Highlights: Gomagoi, Dreisprachespitze

With 48 hairpin bends on one side of Stelvio Pass and 40 on the other, this mountain pass is a challenge to any cyclist. The summit is a shrine to cyclist Fausto Coppi, the great modernizer of the sport in Italy.

Closed in winter and often blocked by snow in early summer, if the twists and turns of the Stelvio Pass don't get you, the altitude will. The road is long enough – over 20 km on either side, but in fact the gradient is not that steep. Your real enemy is the height. As you climb, the proportion of oxygen in the air falls, putting extra strain on the heart and circulation. The body's capacity really starts to decline above 2,400 metres (7,874 ft) – and the Stelvio peaks at 2,758 metres. The temperature difference between the bottom and the top can be as much as 20°C.

The Pass was first included in the Giro d'Italia in 1953, and that year Fausto Coppi staged an amazing attack on the race leader Hugo Koblet, 11 km from the summit of the pass. He went on to win not only the stage but the event. Since then the highest stage in the race each year has been named 'Cima Coppi', the Coppi Summit. In the 12 years that the Stelvio has been a stage, it has always taken the accolade – it is the highest paved road in the Eastern Alps.

On one day a year in late August or early September the pass is closed to motor traffic and given over to the 12,000 cyclists who annually take advantage of the clear roads. The whole road is completely closed from December to May, and the rest of the time cyclists must share it with drivers who are probably more nervous than they are about the tight corners.

Most cycle the route from east to west, beginning in Prad in South Tyrol. The road was made in 1825 to link Austria's German-speaking Tyrol region (in which Prad lies) to its new acquisition, Italian-speaking Lombardy (where Bormio sits). In time both Lombardy and South Tyrol became part of Italy; but to this day 97% of Prad's population speaks German. Prato, the Italian name for the town, is only used in official documents and signs.

At Gomagoi the sides of the valley are so close to each other that the houses are built into them. The first four hairpins come before and after the tiny village of Trafoi; then in the last 13 km of the ascent come forty-four more. There are hotels and refreshments at the top and, if you have the energy, the short walk up Dreisprachenspitze (Piz de las Trais Linguas, or 'Three Languages Peak'), which marks the meeting of Tyrol, Lombardy and Switzerland nearby. The descent to Bormio, an ancient spa town and modern ski resort, is beautiful and thrilling. You'll be glad of Bormio's ancient hot springs by the time you get to the bottom. The moment at Spondalunga, when the valley opens up before you at the top of a ladder of fourteen more hairpins, is unforgettable.

OPPOSITE: It may be lung-busting, but cycling glory awaits you at the top of the Stelvio Pass.

Upper Danube Cycle Path

Germany

Length: 600 km, 373 miles
Start: Donaueschingen
Finish: Passau
Highlights: Donaueschingen Spring, Kolbingen Caves, Schloss Werenwag, Sigmaringen, Ulm Minster, Weltenburg Narrows, Kelheim Freedom Hall, Regensburg (and stone bridge), Passau

You can cycle the whole length of the River Danube from the Black Forest to the Black Sea. While most choose the Austrian section from Passau to Vienna, the stretch from its source across southern Germany offers the same gentle gradient and quieter paths.

No other river in the world flows through as many different countries as the Danube: 10 in total. Can you name them all? And the 19 from which it drains its waters? At 2,850 km (1,770 miles) in length it's by far the longest river in Western Europe. From early in its course it acts as a formidable barrier. For a long time it marked the northern extent of the Roman Empire and still acts as border between many of the countries which it irrigates. Its name means simply 'great river'.

A dispute about the real source of the Danube was only resolved in a German court in 1981, in favour of a spring in the grounds of Donaueschingen Castle. The site has been revered since Roman times, and now emerges into a temple-like stone pool, ringed with columns and a statue. So Donaueschingen marks the start of the Upper Danube Cycle Path.

Historically, towns and villages sprang up on riverbanks for one of two reasons: either they took advantage of places where river crossings were easier or more desirable; or they grew up around a defensive position where the river contributed a useful barrier. There are 324 bridges over the Danube and probably even more castles along its banks.

Immendingen sits on an ancient trade route and boasts not one but two castles in the town, one of them later used as a foundry and factory with power derived from a weir across the Danube. Nearby in Zimmern there is a fine wooden bridge over the river. Tuttlingen, the next town downstream, was a Roman border post and still has the ruins of a later castle. On a stretch downriver from Immendingen, the Danube can sometimes run dry because of a sinkhole in the riverbed. This water re-emerges at Aachtopf, Germany's largest limestone spring, far to the south, from which it flows into Lake Constance, and therefore into the Rhine.

At Mühlheim, literally 'Mill-Home', there have been watermills since Roman times. Its castle is built on the steep sides of the river where it has eroded wide bends through a large outcrop of limestone.

Almost everywhere on the Upper Danube is similarly fascinating: a rich mixture of natural beauty and aeons of history. Look out for Schloss Werenwag high on a clifftop on the

TOP: Now considered to be the source of the Danube, the spring at Donaueschingen.

ABOVE: The cycle path east of Neuburg, Bavaria.

OPPOSITE: Schloss Sigmaringen at Baden-Württemberg.

way to Sigmaringen, the ancient seat of the Hohenzollern dynasty which ruled Prussia, Germany and Romania. The family still owns the spectacular castle which dominates the town.

Gradually the valley opens out and the river widens; castles become palaces and crossings become even more important. Further downstream, Ulm is the highest navigable point on the river for small vessels. The church spire in its ancient centre is reputedly the highest in the world at 161 metres (528 ft). The Danube here crosses from the province of Baden-Württemberg into Bavaria, with all its fine regional cuisine and world-famous beers.

At Donauwörth, roughly halfway to Passau, modern flood defences are an indication of the

dangers as well as the benefits that a powerful river can bring. Ingolstadt, today a modern town and the headquarters of Audi and Airbus, has a fictional history as the town where Mary Shelley's Baron Frankenstein created his monster. Its New Castle was built in the fourteenth century, and it still has some of its original town gates. After the Weltenburg Narrows (a deep gorge with a monastery in the bottom), Kelheim is dominated by the extraordinary Befreiungshalle, 'Freedom Hall'. This huge cylindrical monument was built by Ludwig I of Bavaria to celebrate victory over Napoleon here in 1815.

The urban jewel in the Upper Danube crown is Regensburg, a surviving medieval town without equal. Its twelfth-century bridge, still used by cyclists, was crossed by crusaders on their way

TOP: Schloss Neuburg alongside the Danube (Donau) in Neuburg an der Donau.

ABOVE: Weltenburg Abbey at Kelheim.

to the Holy Land. A building which opened as the workers' canteen during the construction of the bridge claims to be the oldest restaurant in the world still in continuous use: today it is the Regensburg Sausage Kitchen. The city's ancient centre suffered little damage during World War II despite the presence nearby of an aircraft factory, and today it is a UNESCO World Heritage Site with 1,500 listed buildings. Straubing, another historical centre, hosts many events including a jazz festival and one of the largest beer festivals in the region.

And finally, the cycle path rolls into Passau. Here the Danube is joined from left and right by the substantial Ilz and Inn rivers, so the town has always been a key defensive and trade centre. A thirteenth-century fortress, the Veste Oberhaus, overlooks the city and the old quarter at the point where all three rivers meet. Soaked in history, today it's a modern university town and a centre for cruises up and down the Danube.

The Danube Cycle Path is part of a much longer route, EuroVelo 6, which runs from the mouth of the Loire on France's Atlantic Coast to the mouth of the Danube on the Black Sea. Nine of the EuroVelo routes devised by the European Union pass through Germany. The Danube Path is just one of 37 designated German national riverside cycle trails. Among the rivers cyclable are the Rhine; the Elbe (described in part elsewhere in this book); the Main, which starts in the

mountains of northern Bavaria and flows through Würzburg and Frankfurt to join the Rhine near Wiesbaden; and the Altmühl, which carves deep gorges in the Bavarian mountains before joining the Danube at Kelheim. The Moselle in western Germany is a vineyard-lined tributary of the Rhine, and another Rhine tributary, the Neckar, used to carry Black Forest timber to the river port of Heilbronn through castle-lined gorges.

TOP LEFT: The Hall of Liberation (1837) on the hill above Kelheim, a project commissioned by King Ludwig I.

TOP RIGHT: Medieval houses on the banks of the river at Regensburg.

ABOVE: Journey's end in Passau.

Vasco-Navarro Greenway

Spain

Length: 92 km, 57 miles
Start: Vitoria-Gasteiz
Finish: Estella
Highlights: Sierra de Elgea, Villarreal de Álava Station, Landa, Otazu Station, Estíbaliz Sanctuary, Trokoniz Tunnel, Santo Toribio Chapel, Atauri Viaduct, River Berrón/Ega, Antoñana, Arquijas Viaduct and Tunnel, Estella Picudo Bridge

It took 45 years to build and was closed down in 1967 after only 40 years of service. The Vasco-Navarro line ceased to be profitable in the 1950s, but today the route is a gentle bike ride on tarmac and packed earth through the mountains and gorges, villages and towns of the Basque Country.

The original route of the Vasco-Navarro Railway ran 139 km from Estella to Mekolalde north of Vitoria-Gasteiz. País Vasco-Navarro was the nineteenth-century term for the Basque Country; and you'll find that places along the route have two names, one in Spanish and the other in the Basque language. Several sections of the old track bed are now in regular leisure use and more will join them. Beside the sections around Vitoria-Gasteiz, a detached spur of the route near its northern terminus has also been restored as a bike trail. That part runs up the Artixa valley to Oñati, where a Basque university was founded in 1540.

Vitoria-Gasteiz was the European Union's first Green Capital in 2012 and a UNESCO Global Green City in 2019. It has an excellent network of bike paths, and is ringed by the Vuelta al Anillo Verde, the Green Belt Bikeway. That connects the 13-km stretch north of the city with the almost continuous 79-km line to Estella.

Vitoria-Gasteiz is the capital of the Basque Country. It's a lively, modern city with a charming medieval centre. The Duke of Wellington is something of a celebrity here thanks to his victory at the Battle of Vitoria in 1813, which led to the French forces being driven out of Spain and subsequent victory in the Peninsular War, and is commemorated with a statue in the city's Virgen Blanca Square. An English company, the Anglo Vasco Navarro Railway Company, built some of the early sections of the line before going bankrupt in 1914.

The trail immediately north of Vitoria-Gasteiz was the first to be turned into a bike trail. It leaves the city from Gamarra Park, heading straight as an arrow across a wide agricultural landscape at the base of the Sierra de Elgea. Many of the old railway buildings survive: most are homes or restaurants now. In the middle of nowhere the dilapidated station of Villarreal de Álava stands beside the old electricity substation which powered the line when it was electrified.

As the line begins to climb the foothills of the Sierra de Elgea it runs through forests of oak, alder and beech. The trail passes close to the village of Landa and the Ullíbarri-Gamboa

TOP: Plaza de la Virgen Blanca in Vitoria-Gasteiz.

ABOVE: Skirting the Ullíbarri-Gamboa Reservoir near Vitoria-Gasteiz.

OPPOSITE: Vineyards line the road near Echauri.

Reservoir, a popular recreation area for *babazorros* ('bean sacks'), as the citizens of Vitoria-Gasteiz are known. There are other bike trails here, and the main route ends a few kilometres further on at the entrance to Arlabán Pass at the western end of the Aizkorri-Aratz National Park.

The longer section to Estella leaves from the south of the city. The bike paths across Vitoria-Gasteiz are painted red and known as *bidegorris* ('red paths' in Basque). Signs lead you to the Esmaltaciones roundabout in the south-east where you join the old track bed towards Estella. At first it runs straight and true like the northern leg, across open fields.

If the buildings of the line have a pleasing uniformity, it's thanks to Alejandro Mendizábal, the line's chief engineer and architect. Otazu Station, for example, sits with its pretty balcony and porch just across the bridge over the Arga river. It's now a tourist hostel.

A 2-km spur from the line is worth following. It leads to the Sanctuary of Nuestra Señora de Estíbaliz, a hostel for pilgrims on the Santiago Way since the tenth century. The present eleventh-century building is a Romanesque gem, and it's a sign of the place's holy significance that it received its own station when the Vasco-Navarro Railway was constructed.

Back on the main trail, the line maintains its level run with the help of embankments, cuttings and, at Trokoniz, a tunnel. Cuttings through the foothills of the Alavesa mountains were a regular problem for the railway, often blocked with snow in the winter. After Erentxun, with its ruined station, the line starts to climb and its character changes from straight lines to hillside curves and from open fields to woodland.

The railway plunges into the Laminoria Tunnel (2,250 metres/7,381 ft) beneath the Ullíbarri Pass. When the teams digging it from both ends met in the middle, they were only seven centimetres out of alignment. Unfortunately cave-ins and flooding have made the tunnel impassable for cyclists, who must instead take an 8-km detour around it on the Guereñu Pass. This is by far the toughest section of the Vasco-Navarro Greenway, with gradients of up to 17%.

You rejoin the trackbed by a humble chapel dedicated to Santo Toribio. In the forested hills of

BELOW: More vineyards, this time outside Laguardia, with the Sierra de Cantabria mountains in the distance.

BOTTOM LEFT: A great use for old railway carriages, repurposed as an information centre for the trail, at Antoñana.

BOTTOM RIGHT: The Arquijas viaduct at Álava.

Laminoria the trail passes pretty Cicujano, with its circular church, before going through the short, curving Leorza tunnel. In Maeztu, a larger village than most on the trail, the station has been occupied by local government offices. Beyond Maeztu the hills squeeze the road, railway and River Berrón tightly together at the foot of the Peña las Cinco mountain. At Atauri the trail crosses a seven-arch viaduct before tunnelling under Monte del Fraile, and at Antoñana some old railway carriages have become an information centre about the route. The old walled village here is famous for its honey.

As the valley turns sharply to the left, the Berrón river changes its name to the Ega, passing the local hub of Santa Cruz de Campezo. The route leaves the river briefly to squeeze through the narrow Arquijas Pass. It emerges briefly on a magnificent 30-metre-high (98 ft) nine-arch viaduct before plunging into the 1,400-metre/4,593-ft Arquijas Tunnel. From here on, the Ega guides cyclists to Estella.

Estella, like Vitoria-Gasteiz, has grown over the years since the railway's closure, and the last few kilometres are on new paths. Estella often hosts the Grand Prix Miguel Induráin, a one-day cycle race named for the five-times Tour de France-winning Spanish cyclist. The town grew up around an important river-crossing point on the Camino de Santiago, and the wealth generated by pilgrims is evident in the fine church and palace architecture of the town – in the fifteenth century the town was known as Estella the Elegant. There are plenty of facilities and accommodation for today's pedalling pilgrims at the end of the Vasco–Navarro Line.

RIGHT: Gazing out across the rooftops of Estella.

Voie Verte, Burgundy

France

Length: 70 km, 43 miles
Start: Chalon-sur-Saône
Finish: Mâcon
Highlights: Chalon Museum, Givry Grain Market, Buxy, Cluny Abbey, Berzé-le-Châtel Castle, Mâcon Bridge

France has a highly developed network of cycle routes, all graded according to precise standards of provision and difficulty. The country's *voies vertes* – 'green ways' – are completely traffic-free, and one route in Burgundy is a distillation of all that is good in France.

Voies vertes are generally near but not within towns and cities, over relatively short distances and designed for days out.

The first ever voie verte was laid out in southern Burgundy, a gentle landscape ideal for cycling. It ran initially from the vineyards of Givry to the magnificent abbey at Cluny, and now, extended at either end, it runs from Chalon-sur-Saône to Mâcon. It runs across the Côte Chalonnaise, a hillside covered in vines; and the 70-km run can be converted into a loop by returning on a *voie bleue*, a riverside path along the Saône.

Chalon, with a history going back at least to Roman times, was the birthplace of Nicéphore Niépce, a pioneer in photography. A museum in the town also displays his 1807 Pyréolophore – the world's first internal combustion engine – and his 1818 take on the bicycle, for which he coined the word *vélocipède*. Where better to start a bicycle ride!

The route heads west to Givry with its unusual circular grain market, then south past the pretty, unspoilt village of Buxy. The historic highlight of the route is Cluny Abbey, the torchbearer for Benedictine monasticism in Europe for over 800 years until it was destroyed during the French Revolution. Dedicated to St Peter, its original church was the largest in the world until construction began on St Peter's in the Vatican.

South of Cluny the route passes Berzé-le-Châtel, a handsome turreted fortress once ruled by a troubadour and now open to the public. The trail continues through a chilly 1,600-metre (5,250-ft) tunnel (with an overland alternative) and ends in Mâcon, a river port in prehistoric times, which the Romans subsequently developed. Today it's the busy capital of the Saône-et-Loire Department, with a handsome waterfront and a fine eleven-arched bridge over the river.

There is a plan to link several voies vertes in Burgundy to form an 800-km Tour de Bourgogne. If they're all as relaxed and beautiful as this one, it will be a tour worth undertaking.

OPPOSITE TOP: A statue of Nicéphore Niépce, the man often credited with having invented photography, in Chalon-sur-Saône.

BELOW: The castle at Berzé-le-Châtel.

BOTTOM: A panorama of the Saône river at Mâcon.

Whistler A-Line Singletrack

British Columbia, Canada

Length: 2.4 km, 1.5 miles
Start/Finish: Whistler Mountain Bike Park

The Whistler Mountain Bike Park in British Columbia is an MTB thrill-seeker's paradise in the forests of Canada's Coast Mountains. Its black-diamond-rated A-Line run is five minutes of gravity-fuelled, adrenalin-inducing intensity.

The Park is at Whistler Blackcomb, the largest and most popular ski resort in North America. The area was first developed in a bid for the 1968 Winter Olympics and, although it didn't win that year, did host the Games in 2010. Eleven of its 25 lifts are able to operate in the summer months too, something that adventurous MTB riders were quick to take advantage of.

Today the Bike Park covers four distinct zones including the recently opened Creekside Zone, served by gondolas and chairlifts. On the latter, every other chair is replaced by a bike rack. There are around 50 trails on over 250 km of routes for all levels of ability, with a maximum drop of 1,100 metres (3,609 ft) from the top of the highest zone to the base station.

The original A-Line course began to take shape over the summer of 1998, weaving a naturally flowing trail down through the trees. Some say it was the very first flow trail, the one which inspired every other. Over the years it has grown, and continues to grow, with the addition of built elements, banked turns and longer sightlines to improve visibility and anticipation. Near the bottom there's now a huge jump, or booter; and

throughout the run, riders spend nearly as much time in the air as on the ground.

All the trails in Whistler Mountain Bike Park are graded for difficulty, in one of five categories. Surprisingly, given its reputation, the A-Line falls into the advanced, Black Diamond class – above Green Circle beginner runs and Blue Square intermediates, but below Double Black Diamond (Expert Only) and Red Triangle routes, which are strictly for the hardcore and professionals.

Routes are also classified as Freeride (like the A-Line) on man-made trails with added items like ride-ons, jumps and wallrides; and Technical, which use natural features such as rocks, drops and tree roots and demand much more from the rider in the way of MTB skills. In total there are only four pro trails and just two freeride double-diamond routes ranked tougher than the A-Line.

In addition, there's a special area of pro-level jumps and drops, with testing gaps and airs,

called the Boneyard Slopestyle Course. The Boneyard is used only during the park's annual Crankworx competitive festival of freeride biking. It's the largest such event in North America and, like the A-Line itself, has inspired others around the world.

OPPOSITE: The much-loved A-Line is two categories below the toughest trails at Whistler.

BELOW LEFT: Downtown Whistler buzzes all year round.

BELOW: Remember to take your GoPro to relive the experience.

White Rim Trail, Moab

Utah, USA

Length: 100 miles, 161 km
Start/Finish: Canyonlands National Park Visitor Center
Highlights: Musselman Arch, Airport Tower Butte, Washer Woman Arch, White Crack, Murphy Hogback, Black Crack, Candlestick Tower, Fort Bottom

A road engineered in the 1950s at the height of the Cold War to provide access for uranium prospectors now forms a dramatic leisure trail in the red rock wilderness between the Green River and the Colorado.

Grand County, Utah, is well named. This is canyon country, and its capital, Moab, makes an excellent centre for a cycling holiday. To the north lie the two thousand stone arches of the Arches National Park; to the east are the La Sal Mountains, capped by 12,306-ft (3,751-metre) Mount Waas; and to the west, framed by the Colorado and its tributary the Green River, is Canyonlands National Park.

These vast, empty landscapes have been popular locations for Hollywood. Well over 50 films have been shot there or thereabouts, from John Wayne's *Stagecoach* to Johnny Depp's *Lone Ranger*. The whole county is criss-crossed with trails popular with hikers, cyclists and 4x4 enthusiasts. The two rivers are centres for kayaking and white-water rafting. There are hundreds of miles of MTB tracks including the celebrated Slickrock Trail and the White Rim Trail.

Moab's boom years were in the mid-twentieth century, when rich deposits of uranium, vanadium, potash, manganese, oil and gas were discovered to the south of the town. The Atomic Energy Commission (AEC) had been stockpiling uranium for nuclear weapons in the Cold War with the USSR. In the hope of finding further deposits the AEC built the White Rim Road to encourage mining companies to prospect the lands to the west. None were found and all the mines closed, leaving the dusty unmade road for the benefit of all.

The White Rim Road gets its name from the exposed geological layer of white sandstone that

ABOVE: The winding Shafer Canyon Road descends for an exhilarating 18 miles, but 4x4s use it too.

LEFT: Musselman Arch near the White Rim Trail.

it follows. The layer lies at the base of the Island in the Sky, a high plateau at the heart of the Canyonlands National Park. The road tracks the distinctive white rock in a large horseshoe, down the Colorado valley and then upstream beside the Green River.

The White Rim Trail starts near the Canyonlands Visitor Center 32 miles south-west of Moab. Setting out along the winding Shafer Trail you immediately climb through a succession of steep hairpins to the junction with Potash Road, where the trail proper begins. Not too far along, a short walk from the trail to Gooseneck Overlook gives

you your first glimpse of the Colorado River in the canyon below.

Back on your bike, another five miles will take you past Musselman Arch; not all the arches are in Arches National Park, and in another ten miles you'll see Washer Woman Arch to your right. Before then Lathrop Canyon opens up on the

RIGHT: A clear visual reminder as to how the White Rim Trail got its name.

BELOW: One of the finest views in any American National Park, the Gooseneck on the Colorado River.

left; through it a difficult four-mile trail gives you the only access to the Colorado River from the White Rim.

Just beyond Lathrop stands the unmistakable monolith of Airport Tower Butte, like something straight out of the film *Close Encounters of the Third Kind*. As the trail continues to wind southwards there are views of Buck Canyon, Gooseberry Canyon and the vast Monument Basin, a bend in the Colorado with towering craggy pinnacles like the unfinished sculptures of giants.

There are designated campsites every ten miles or so along the route. Most are beside the trail, but White Crack at the most southerly point of the White Rim is down a 1.5-mile spur. It's worth a detour to get the view of both rivers and the Maze, a crazy network of banded canyons off to your right. This is one of the two highest points on the ride.

The other is the Murphy Hogback, a punishing climb and descent which marks the halfway point about eight miles north of White Crack. Now the route shadows the Green River. Look out for Black Crack, a 300-yard-long, narrow and very deep fissure in the rock table, which you should on no account allow yourself to be tempted to leap. You'll also see the striking profile of the Turk's Head Butte framed by greenery in a tight bend of the river; and then Candlestick Tower, a three-tiered butte a little further on.

After the Potato Bottom campsite, a spur leads down to the ruins of Fort Bottom. The Fort, atop a butte, is actually an ancient Native American tower. Below it at the end of the spur are the remains of a pioneer's log cabin. You may well feel that you are travelling in his or her footsteps.

Back on the trail there's one last and well-named climb, up Hardscrabble Hill. For part of the final five miles you are at last riding along the bank

of the Green River, before the White Rim Trail officially ends where you join Mineral Bottom Road. From here, after an initial, shockingly steep hairpin climb, it's a relatively straightforward ride up over the Island in the Sky back to the start.

Access to the White Rim Trail is limited to one hundred users per day: fifty cyclists and fifty 4x4s, who must apply for permits for both day use and for overnight camping. The size of groups using the trail is also regulated: three motor vehicles may travel together, and up to fifteen cyclists, and their departure times are controlled to keep groups apart and reduce the hazard of dust. Half of all permits are available to book in advance, and half are issued on the day. There is, at the time of writing, no charge for day use over and above the fee for entrance to the National Park; there is a charge for overnight camping, however, and no campfires are allowed.

You can complete the trail in a long hard day, but it's worth taking longer with one of the managed tours available. Tours can take from two to four days to complete the rigorous route. A tour organizer will assist with camping facilities and, most importantly, with supplies of water carried in a support vehicle. Despite the presence of two major white-water rivers near the route, no drinking water is available throughout its length.

ABOVE RIGHT: Turk's Head Butte on the Green River.

RIGHT: The fearsome 'Black Crack'. Jumping over it is not advised, but tempting.

The Whole Enchilada Singletrack

Utah, USA

Length: 35 miles, 56 km
Start: Haystack Mountain
Finish: Moab
Highlights: Burro Pass, Warner Lake, Mason Draw, Round Mountain, Castle Valley, Grandstaff Canyon

The Whole Enchilada is just that. It drops 8,000 ft (2,438 metres) through three distinct climate zones, and the temperature can double from top to bottom. It starts with a 600-ft (180-metre), 5% ascent, and the terrain varies from meadowland to tyre-shredding loose rock. How hungry are you?

You've got to be hungry to take on the Whole Enchilada. This is no light snack of a trail. It could easily take you over six hours to complete it, excluding the time it takes to get to the remote starting point high in the La Sal Mountains, so the first tip is to start early and avoid the heat of the day. In high summer, temperatures in the lower part of the trail can reach 100°F (37°C). In the winter the upper stages of the route are closed – the highest point is 11,168 ft (3,404 metres) above sea level – and even in August the temperature can fall to 40°F (4°C) after sundown.

The Whole Enchilada strings together several shorter trails to the east of Moab. It is well signposted (as W.E.) and it begins from a car park behind Haystack Mountain, about an hour's drive out of town. After a short, gentle path across grassland it starts to climb sharply over loose stone chips towards the summit of Burro Pass between Haystack and Manns Peak. This is the highpoint of the trail but not the end of the climbing. After four miles of downhill the path levels off as it passes Warner Lake and camping area, then climbs again at the start of the Hazard County section of the W.E. Here, the welcome shade of the aspen forest ends; from now on the trail is through scrub and desert.

There is no water supply throughout the Whole Enchilada, but where you cross the La Sal Loop Road there is a toilet, just to the north of the Mason Spring Campground. It can still snow here in May. The route continues beyond the road as the Kokopelli Trail, but if you're pressed for time you can take the Loop Road back to town.

If you want an easier ride for a while you can take the Jimmy Keen Trail on the left just beyond the road. It adds about five miles to the route but is all gentle downhill flow. Jimmy Keen rejoins the W.E. at a crossroads where it joins the Upper Porcupine Singletrack. This is a dizzying bedrock section on the edge of a steep drop from Porcupine Rim to the Mason Draw valley to the north.

From the Rim you can see the buttes of Castle Valley ahead of you. As you draw level with Round Mountain in the middle of the valley, the trail veers away from the Rim and makes its way at last down to the Colorado River at Grandstaff Canyon. From here it's an easy road ride back to Moab. The Whole Enchilada is a trail for the technically experienced MTB-er. Bring sunscreen, a repair kit and plenty of food and water, and the rewards will be some of the best views from any rugged trail in the world.

TOP: La Sal Mountain Loop Road.

ABOVE: Moab has many more heart-stopping singletracks when you're through with the Enchilada.

OPPOSITE: The view from Porcupine Rim.

Yungas Road

Bolivia

Length: 64 km, 40 miles
Start: La Cumbre Pass
Finish: Coroico
Highlights: Laguna Estrellani, Río Elena, Mono Zip-Line, Coroico

You can do this the easy way, or the hard way. Either way it's best you don't suffer from vertigo. The Yungas Road, built through mountainous terrain to supply troops on the frontline during a war between Bolivia and Paraguay, is all downhill for over 60 km. Or all up.

This is the 'Most Dangerous Road in the World', according to the Inter-American Development Bank, who declared it so in 1995. Clinging perilously to the vertiginous slopes of the Andes, it twists and turns its way down from La Cumbre Pass to the town of Coroico, which was isolated from the rest of Bolivia before the road was engineered in the 1930s. The height difference between the two is about 3,500 metres (11,483 ft).

Sections of the road were widened in the late twentieth century and a new highway bypassing the most dangerous sections was opened in 2006. In that year, 300 people lost their lives on the Yungas Road, where – if you miss a hairpin bend – the drop can be as much as 660 metres (2,165 ft) into the dense vegetation of the valley below. The road is lined in places with memorials to those who didn't make it. The surface is dangerous in wet weather and in places, where the road has been engineered beneath overhangs, you may find yourself riding behind waterfalls. No wonder locals prefer to cross the valleys on zip-wires.

The easy way starts in La Paz, Bolivia's capital, from where minibuses carry cycling tourists and their bikes up to the top of La Cumbre Pass, 1,000 metres (3,281 ft) higher than the city and 23 km to the east. From there it is an exhilarating freewheel ride around the valleys of the rivers Pongo, Unduavi, Elena and Yolosa. If you dare take your eyes off the road, the views are breathtaking. Coroico, at the descent's conclusion, is a pretty town with a fine central square and plenty of hostels for the traveller.

The hard way, of course, is to start in Coroico. Motorized traffic is currently banned from the worst sections of the road, saving many lives in the process and making it considerably safer for the thousands of cyclists who tackle the route every year. If you do choose to do it as a climb, there is a lake and café waiting for you at La Cumbre, where you can catch your breath and congratulate yourself before enjoying the 23 km down to La Paz.

The uphill direction is the route of the annual Skyrace, an extreme event for cyclists and runners. If you think that completing the distance competitively may not be for you, bear in mind that in 2019 Mirtha Munoz, one of the founders of the Skyrace, became the oldest woman to complete it by bicycle, at the age of 70.

ABOVE: A tour party downs bikes and contemplates the vertiginous view.

OPPOSITE: 'El Camino de la Muerte', the road of death, is actually a lot safer for cyclists than motorists, but safety doesn't add to its cachet.